# THE POWER
## *of the*
# AWAKENED HUMAN

*A Practical Guide to Conscious Reality Creation*

ILDIKO OLAH

Copyright © 2024 by Ildiko Olah

All rights reserved. No part of this book may be reproduced or transmitted in any form or by any means, including photocopying, recording or other electronic or mechanical methods without the written permission of the publisher, except in the case of brief quotations embedded in critical articles and reviews, and certain other non-commercial uses permitted by copyright law.

This material has been written and published for educational purposes only. The author and the publisher shall have neither liability nor responsibility to any person or entity with respect to any loss, damage or injury caused or alleged to be caused directly or indirectly by the information contained within this book.

Cover design by Eva Major

ISBN: 978-1-7383342-0-9

## ACKNOWLEDGEMENTS

I'm very grateful to all the people who have contributed to the birth of this book. I could not have done it without their help with editing, the technical aspects of publishing and the words of encouragement I received while writing. My heartfelt thanks to my family and friends, especially Kerry Grbich, Iren Horvath, Csilla Vagasi and my husband Zsolt.

I'd like to express my gratitude to my teachers as well: all the courageous lightworkers who are well known and those who are not, who have been speaking their truth for decades and helped people like me discover our true nature and purpose.

I would also like to thank my non-physical team for standing behind me and supporting me all through my life, guiding me towards writing this book, and lighting the way for me throughout the entire process.

A special thanks goes to Eva Major whose beautiful artwork graces the cover of my book.

# CONTENTS

**Introduction** .................................................... 1

**Chapter 1**
THE BASIC CONCEPTS ...................................... 7
   The Shift in Consciousness ............................... 7
   Life Plans, Contracts and Challenges .................... 9
   Probable Realities .......................................... 15
   Duality ....................................................... 18
   Awakened and Conscious ................................. 20
   Conscious Reality Creation ............................... 22

**Chapter 2**
VIBRATION AND FREQUENCY ......................... 26

**Chapter 3**
CREATING A HIGH VIBRATIONAL
REALITY ........................................................ 35

**Chapter 4**
THE TOOLS OF CONSCIOUS REALITY
   CREATION ................................................... 46
     Intent ...................................................... 47
     Beliefs .................................................... 48
     Focus ..................................................... 50
     Visualization ............................................ 35

Manifestation .......................................... 61
Using the Innate .................................... 67
Meditation ............................................. 69
Dropping Expectations ............................ 73
Acceptance ........................................... 76
Being present ....................................... 78
Affirmations ......................................... 81

## Chapter 5
MORE TOOLS AND PRACTICES OF
CONSCIOUS REALITY CREATION ............... 86
Positive Attitude ..................................... 86
Eliminating Limiting Beliefs ...................... 89
No Judgement ........................................ 90
Overcoming Past Conditioning .................... 91
Verbalization ......................................... 93
Self Observation ..................................... 94
Communicating with the Non-physical .......... 97
Choosing the Company We Keep ................. 99
The Taming of the Ego ............................ 100
Live and Let Live .................................. 102
Knowing Your Power .............................. 103
Non-interference .................................... 105
Minding Your Energy ............................. 108
Accepting and Appreciating Yourself ........... 109
Using High Vibrational Solutions ................ 111

**Chapter 6**
THE BENEFITS OF CONSCIOUS, HIGH
VIBRATIONAL LIVING ……..…………….…. 114

**Chapter 7**
MASS CONSCIOUSNESS ………….…..…..… 118

**Chapter 8**
HOW I KEEP MY VIBRATION HIGH ……..…. 125

**Chapter 9**
HOW I CREATE MY REALITY
CONSCIOUSLY ………………..…..………… 130

**Chapter 10**
THE REQUIREMENTS OF LEARNING AND
PRACTISING CONSCIOUS REALITY
CREATION ..………………………………..…… 134

**Chapter 11**
CO-CREATING WITH THE UNIVERSE …….. 141

**Chapter 12**
PRACTICAL EXAMPLES AND TIPS FOR
CONSCIOUS REALITY CREATION …………. 144

**Chapter 13**
COMMON QUESTIONS AMONG THOSE
WALKING THE PATH OF AWAKENING ........ 164

**Chapter 14**
FINAL WORDS ........................................ 206

ABOUT THE AUTHOR .............................. 208

# INTRODUCTION

I was sitting on the couch, listening to Christmas music one January afternoon when I suddenly realized what I was supposed to do. After spending so many years feeling a strong urge to do something but not knowing what, and being so restless and frustrated, the revelation brought with it a sense of surrender and relief.

All this began 20 years ago when I had my first spiritual experience on one of the hiking trails of Arizona. It was the pivotal event that started me on my journey of spiritual awakening and resulted in the changing of the way I look at myself, the world around me, and the way I relate to life. Or rather, it opened my eyes to how *life relates to me*. Yes, that is quite a difference. I believe that if everyone knew and understood how life relates to us and not just the other way around, humanity's circumstances of living would change for the better very quickly.

But let's go back to Arizona for a moment. My husband and I had taken the very first of our numerous road trips to the US that year, and this being back in 2002 we enjoyed visiting many sights and hiking trails before the crowds descended on all these places a few years later. This most memorable trail is on Navajo territory and is named Canyon de Chelly National Monument. It is not far from the well known tourist spot that is the Spider Rock Overlook, and features ruins built into the great red rocks by the ancestral Pueblo Indians.

On that hot, July morning we trekked down the winding trail into the canyon. We found ourselves surrounded by towering red rocks all around, and led by a red dirt path lined with high grown bushes, their branches creating a canopy over us. A red coloured muddy creek ran through the canyon, and as we walked we were struck by a sense of peace and reverence that filled us both. The place felt absolutely magical, and we spent some time just taking and breathing it all in. As we walked on we heard animal sounds, and ended up at a chicken wire fence that separated the trail side of the canyon from the area where present day Navajos lived, growing corn and raising livestock. As we were peeping through, listening to the sounds of dogs barking and goats bleating, suddenly a native began drumming and singing just out of view. In that moment I found myself transported back in time, and I was gripped by the feeling that I knew this place, I've been here before, I *lived* here before! It was such a profound feeling, a deep inner knowledge that burned inside me, bright as a sun. I stood there transfixed, reveling in the sensation, when a family with a couple of young children walked up behind us talking loudly and the illusion shattered. I was suddenly back in the present, feeling quite a bit bewildered and ever so disappointed that it was over. I looked at my husband who was standing next to me and was completely unaware of this incredible experience I've just had and said to him, "You will never believe what just happened to me!"

After we got home from our trip I sat down to research reincarnation, life after death and out of body experiences. This lead me to further study astral travel, projection of consciousness, and most importantly, meditation. That was not an easy task for me to learn, having had a head full of thoughts all the time at that point in my life. I was constantly mind chatting, monkey talking, singing, daydreaming in every minute of my waking hours. So it was difficult to keep my mind empty but once I mastered it, my goodness! It was as if a switch had been turned on. My third eye opened and I began to have all kinds of incredible psychic experiences. Visions, projections of consciousness that I called time travel, remote viewing, clairvoyance, clairaudience, precognitive dreams, etc. Every meditation brought new adventures and I was so elated by it all, because I realized through these experiences that I was so much more than just a body of flesh and blood I always believed myself to be. And thus my journey of discovering my true nature and the nature of reality had begun. Throughout my search I learned from many others who have been way ahead of me in their knowledge and experience, some well known while others not at all. I'm grateful to them all for sharing their knowledge and assisting me in my own self discovery.

The years of psychic adventures and the studying of the nature of reality was one of the most exciting periods of my life. It changed me to such a degree that in a decade and a half I barely recognized myself. Gone was the monkey talk, the worries and the changing moods, and a general sense of peace and contentment took their place. It was as if I had been put into neutral, or so to speak. But as these changes slowly solidified throughout the years, it seemed that my third eye also slowly began to close. The psychic experiences gradually stopped, meditating became fruitless and I felt a strong sense of loss. I finally realized that I was so much greater than my old 3D self, and now I was cut off from my extra sight and my multidimensional adventures. I called this period the Spiritual Dead Zone.

I was in this frustrating zone for about seven years, during which time I tried to figure out what happened. Why did I lose my ability to shift my consciousness into other realities? Why was I shown what I can be and then have it all taken away? To make things worse, along with the loss of my psychic abilities I had also seemed to have lost my passion and my creativity. I used to have so many hobbies; did crafts, played music and read many books. I was interested in so many things and now I felt completely uninspired. What happened to me?

The answer came to me eventually, but ever so slowly. At one point I began to realize that I needed time to integrate all that I have learned during this incredible period in my life. I had to digest it, let it settle, let it make sense, and I had to learn to apply what I learned in my everyday life. I was going through a transitional period. Once I understood this a lot of the frustration went away, because I knew that by doing all that I was preparing myself for something new. I was getting ready to do something I felt the need to do for years, I just didn't know what that was.

I am a lightworker, like millions of others living on Earth right now. All of us are doing our part in assisting humanity in raising our frequency so we can all ascend to higher dimensions. Many of us are healers, teachers, or working in other positions to serve humanity. Some do this work consciously while others unconsciously. I have felt as if I was a teacher for a long time, I just had no idea what I was supposed to teach and how.

This brings me back to that afternoon in the middle of January, sitting on the couch listening to Christmas music, telling my husband how listening to the cheerful, upbeat music keeps me in high vibration. As soon as those words left my lips I experienced a moment of illumination and I suddenly knew. This is what I'm supposed to teach because this is what I know! I have been learning about frequency, vibration, and their effect on physical reality for many years. I have studied and observed them, experimented with them, and I could clearly see how it all worked in my everyday life. Upon realizing this I felt intense relief, and finally, a sense of new purpose in my life. This is what I'm here for, to teach and show others how to consciously create their reality! I'm writing this book in the hope that it will help my readers open their eyes at the ways their vibration directly affects their life, and teach them how their frequency is creating their reality and not the other way around. With the help of practical tips, suggestions and personal examples, I endeavour to enable and encourage the readers to take the reins into their own hands when it comes to creating a peaceful and fulfilling life for themselves.

*Chapter 1*

## THE BASIC CONCEPTS

Before we can learn about how to create our reality awake and aware, I'd like the readers to familiarize themselves with some of the basic concepts that lay the foundations for conscious reality creation. These concepts introduce us to the event that launched the evolution of the consciousness of humanity, explain the source and terms of our existence, and help us explore our multidimensional nature.

### THE SHIFT IN CONSCIOUSNESS

When we look back in time in our history we can see that humanity's consciousness has been operating on a low vibrational level for thousands of years. The reasons for that have been much discussed and written about in spiritual circles. I will not go into it, for that is not what I know or have any personal experience with. I would just like to establish that as a race we have been in the dark for a very long time, and at one point we subconsciously decided that we will shift our consciousness and raise our vibration, working our way up to the higher dimensions. The point at which this decision was made is referred to as the Harmonic Convergence, which happened in the year of 1987. From that point on people began to wake up one by one, and as the decades passed, in much greater numbers.

Anybody who is awake and conscious today can look around among their family, friends and the human population in general and see the signs of awakening everywhere. When I look back at my own history I see how in my youth so many parents still operated by the old playbook. They raised their family the way their own parents raised them whether some things made sense or not, just because that's how things were done and nobody asked questions. The following generation started to ask questions though and that is when things began to change. With growing awareness came the recognition of the mindless nature of the old belief systems, attitudes, patterns and behaviours, and once realized and acknowledged these outdated attributes could be changed.

When we look around the internet we can find large masses of awakening people congregating everywhere, helping, supporting, teaching and learning from each other. We see spiritual workshops and training centres operating everywhere, and new non-traditional healing modalities being invented and put into good use all over the world. We must acknowledge that there are still a lot of dark, low vibrational leaders, organizations and events in the mass reality, but anyone who is willing to look can see that there are clear signs of humanity shifting its worldview, attitude and priorities.

The SHIFT is here. We are right in the middle of it, and this is a train that cannot and will not be stopped. So welcome aboard, take a seat and watch the greatest event in the known human history unfold!

## LIFE PLANS, CONTRACTS AND CHALLENGES

In every hour of every day millions of people all over the world ask the age old question: why are we here? Add to that, who are we, what is the point of our life, and most importantly, what is the meaning of it? Why is life so difficult, why are so many people struggling, and what's with all the pain and suffering in the world? To answer those questions, first we have go back to the most important one:

Who are we?

Dear Reader, we are the ONE. The One Great Consciousness, All That Is, God, the Creator, Source, the Universe. There have been many names given to it throughout history. The One Great Consciousness desired to know itself, so it sent out individualized pieces of itself to create experiences in both physical and non-physical multiverses. There have been many great metaphysical books written about this subject so I just mention it for the purpose of establishing our origin.

What we need to know in order to understand the nature of our reality is that we are all individualized, higher dimensional consciousnesses (or so called consciousness units) and eternal light beings who decided to lower our frequency and express part of ourselves into physical matter. We created for ourselves a multidimensional playground that some people call the holographic universe, others the matrix or the energy field. Since our nature is multidimensional we exist in many dimensions all at once, but due to the very dense nature of 3D the part of us that exists here has no conscious awareness of its quantum nature. That is the reason we have completely forgotten who we are, why we are here, and what we are supposed to be doing.

Why are we here?

We came here to experience life in matter and to learn how to manipulate energy in a physical environment; to create physical bodies, events, objects, plants and animals, see colours, hear sounds, to feel textures, smells and tastes, and to feel and express emotions of all kinds. To put it simply, we came here to LIVE and experience life, so through us The One Consciousness will know itself.

Imagine if you will, how our brain receives information. It doesn't know what an object is like until we look at it with our eyes and touch it with our fingers so it can register the sizes, shapes, colours, textures, temperatures, etc. Our brain depends on our senses to receive information just like the One Consciousness uses us, its individual parts, to experience itself. So in a way, we are God's eyes and fingers!

In order to experience physical reality and manipulate energy and matter we need a physical body, and we have to decide the parameters of our desired existence: should we be born male or female, tall or short, live a life of a rich man or rather, a slave? Should we be healthy or sit in a wheelchair all our life? For the unawakened humans living in this 3D world being poor and unhealthy is perceived as a most unfortunate of circumstances, but for a high dimensional consciousness coming into this rich, exciting playground it is a great opportunity for experimentation and adventure!

Before we are born into physical bodies we create a life plan, a purpose, and with the willing participation of other fellow consciousnesses or light beings we make contracts of cooperation. Imagine that you write yourself a play with you in the starring role. You will also need other characters you are going to interact with: parents, siblings, friends, neighbours, coworkers, etc. Once the stage is set and all the actors are in place the curtain goes up and your play begins. You are born into a physical body to parents you have chosen, and grow up living a life based on the purpose you have set for yourself. The supporting characters come into your life at an agreed upon time and play out their part as per their contract. And thus you spend your life living out your play, and when the curtain goes down you discard the physical body and wake up. You look back at how you fared, and at that time you decide whether you want to go back for another performance or not.

For people who are unaware that they are the planners, creators and executors of their own life and challenges (and that is most people on planet Earth) existence in the 3D realm can be experienced as a great deal of struggle, pain and tragedy. Many find it very difficult to cope with it all and spend a lot of their time living in abject misery. Others do better and some pretty well, but still, most people at one time in their life or another begin to wonder: *"Who am I and what is the point of all this?"* Once they start asking these questions things begin to change.

You see, if you've ever seen a play in a theatre or a movie in the cinema, you know that actors are not the only players in a production. There are also a good number of people working tirelessly behind the curtains to make sure the performance is going as smoothly as possible. So while you are performing your personal play titled 'Living on Earth in the Third Dimension' there are non-physical helpers standing by to assist you, waiting for you to call on them whenever the need arises. If you remain silent they stay back and not interfere, but once you start asking questions or call out for help they will come rushing to assist you.

"Why is that?" you ask. "Why don't they help you from day one, whether you ask or not?"

It is because they respect your wishes and your autonomy. You came into this reality to have your experience all on your own and be helped out when you ask for it. If you were a real actor in a play at a theatre you wouldn't want anyone to interfere unless you forgot your lines, right? You would want to do your own thing.

"But that's not fair, we are suffering!" you say. "Why has God forsaken us?"

You haven't been forsaken. You are being respected and allowed to play out your challenges as per the agreement you made before you were born.

If you came into this 3D playground to experience the life of an abused person for example, you have an agreement with a fellow light being who agreed to be your abuser for their own learning experience. You play your part, the other person does his/hers, and as your life is progressing your challenge is how you deal with it. If you can't resolve the issue you will keep repeating the pattern all your life, and once it's over and you have transitioned out of 3D you may come back for another round to see if you can do better this time. If you find a resolution in the form of forgiveness for example then the contract has been fulfilled, and you can move on and create an abuse free environment for yourself for the rest of your life.

The challenge here is to wake up and become conscious of your part and your responsibility in your life choices and circumstances. When you are awake and conscious and you start working on raising your vibration, you can resolve them. I will talk about personal experiences and solutions later in the book.

Once you begin to wonder and ask what is the point and meaning of life, why you are here, what is your purpose and what are you supposed to do, your background team springs into action and you will find yourself nudged towards the information you seek. You search for and read books, watch media content about spirituality and metaphysics and start meditating. Chances are you may begin to experience psychic phenomena such as clairvoyance, telepathy, projections of consciousness, visions, etc. In other words, you are beginning to wake up! You realize that you are so much more than just this body of flesh and blood and you become aware of your multi-dimensional nature.

As they say, "life is a dream," but at one point you are supposed to wake up. When you finally start asking questions your spiritual alarm clock goes off and you begin your journey towards awakening. You either slowly and gradually or quite suddenly become conscious in your "play," and realize that you are the main character in your own production and you have great control over how it's going to go. Once you recognize your power in the creation of your reality you will seek out information about the many ways, tools and methods of conscious reality creation. Armed with knowledge and past experiences you will begin to create the events of your life fully aware of your role in it.

## PROBABLE REALITIES

As we established before, we live in a multiverse in multiple dimensions, manipulating energies in an infinite number of realities. That means that aside from the *You* that you see in the mirror every day, there are an infinite number of other versions of yourself out there, living an infinite number of lives in many different dimensions. Some of them are almost like the one you know, others are completely different, depending on the countless number of choices you make in a lifetime.

We have all heard about parallel or alternate realities in works of fiction for decades, and now it seems that science is slowly catching up and quantum physicists are finally beginning to talk about our multidimensional nature. The multiverse theory explains that every time we make a choice we create or shift into an alternate reality, where we experience that choice and its consequences. So try to imagine that an infinite number of different *You*s are running around in an infinite number of realities, experiencing an infinite number of lives, based on the thousands of choices you make in every minute of your life. This is important information to remember because it's one of the basic building blocks of conscious reality creation. Whenever you stand before the proverbial fork in the road, remember that while you may take one of them and experience the consequences of choosing that particular road, there are a great number of probable realities out there where you take the other one instead or you turn around and choose to go in a completely different direction. Those probable realities with your different choices all exist in the non-physical, waiting for you to make that choice and shift there.

How do we know those probable realities (probable futures) really exist? We know because people have seen them, myself included. During meditation and in the dream state we can access the quantum field where all these probable realities are "running" next to each other. This is how psychics can foretell things we might experience in the future, by accessing the quantum field and seeing probable realities. Their predictions may not be always accurate, since whichever probable future is experienced by the individual or humanity en masse depends on the level of vibration we are on at a particular time and the choices we make. But the information is out there. We can access it, we just have to learn how to work with it.

Since I record a lot of my dreams I had the opportunity to see things in the quantum field that came true several times. One day I dreamed that I was sitting in a circle with a couple of people I didn't know. We were talking but I didn't remember about what. About two weeks later my family was invited to a barbecue party by the parents of a classmate of one of my sons. At one point we found ourselves sitting in plastic garden chairs in a circle around the barbecue in the company of people we've never met before, eating out of paper plates, and as I felt a sense of déjà vu it suddenly hit me that I've seen this exact scenario in my dream! I didn't recall eating, but the strangers sitting in a circle around me were there.

That was one of the few precognitive dreams I've had that I experienced turning into reality. These are probable realities existing in the quantum field, accessible by those who meditate or by the dreaming person whose consciousness shifted into the non-physical during sleep.

When we work on our conscious reality creation we have to be aware of the existence of probable realities and probable futures. They are out there, vibrating with a certain frequency, waiting for us to match that frequency and shift into them. That is how we create our reality consciously.

# DUALITY

The multiverse was created for the purpose of All That Is knowing itself, by sending out individualized parts of itself into a multidimensional environment to learn and experience. Within this framework there are multiple levels of existence to develop and participate in, with attributes appropriate for each level.

One of the attributes of a 3D (Third Dimensional) physical reality is duality. Duality is when two opposites exist at the same time, such as: long and short, ugly and beautiful, rich and poor, love and hate, and good and bad.

Throughout our lifetime we create a number of events for ourselves to experience. Happenings, that depending on their desirability we call either good or bad. However, within the framework of Creation there are no such distinctions. As far as the Universe is concerned there are just events, actions, emotions and reactions, without any values attached to them. To a higher dimensional consciousness everything is just an experience. It is something that one creates, participates in, processes and releases. Because of the existence of duality in the 3D realm we put value on everything we do, say, feel and generally experience. That is why certain things in life are considered good, pleasant and beautiful, while others the opposite.

My personal experience is that as we become conscious and start raising our vibration and therefore our frequency, duality slowly starts to fade away and the divide between good and bad begins to narrow. The more conscious and aware we are the more we realize that everything is indeed just an experience, something to go through to gain knowledge and wisdom from, and then release. When we add negative values to our experiences we create resistance and lower our vibration.

To release the values that we have added to everything we've ever done, felt, said and participated in all our life seems like a difficult thing to do, but I found that it's a spontaneous process I have been going through. It is happening without me having to work at it. It's a natural consequence of my rising frequency that is responsible for much of the inner peace that is my default setting today.

As you work on keeping yourself aware and conscious while raising your vibration, you too will experience the diminishing need to attach value to your life events. Once you observe and understand how life contracts work, it will be clear that whatever events and emotions people experience, be it "good" or "bad," are either for their own life lessons or someone else's, and they created it for and by themselves.

Of course that doesn't mean that we remain cold and unaffected when we see people around us going through hardship. It is natural and quite high vibrational to feel compassion, empathize and want to help. But while doing so it is a good idea to remember that this person is creating this situation or this event for their own learning or teaching experience, by their own free will, and that should be respected.

## AWAKENED AND CONSCIOUS

What does it mean to be awakened and conscious? For different people it means different things. For some it is the awareness of the holographic nature of our so called "matrix," the presence of evil entities, a cabal and shadow government that has enslaved humanity for many a millennia. It may be the realization of the existence of extraterrestrial beings and their involvement in the history of humanity, the discovery of humanity's hidden past and the knowledge of ancient cultures that have been kept from us. For others - including myself - it is the understanding of our multidimensional nature, our connection to the non-physical dimensions, and our ability to create our reality based on our vibration and frequency. Although all of the above is part of our awakening, my focus during the last twenty years has been concentrated on humanity's multidimensional nature. This includes connecting with our inner self and learning and experimenting with the different methods of mastering this holographic matrix we chose to be born into.

There are multiple levels of dimensions in the multiverse, both physical and non-physical, and we have focuses (lives) in all of them. The one you are reading this book in is called 3D, a low vibrational, dense environment, difficult to exist in and navigate until one becomes consciously aware. What adds to our difficulties is that because of the dense nature of this dimension we forget our connection to the spiritual plane every time we incarnate. This amnesia follows us throughout our lives until we either ascend to higher frequencies where the information becomes available, or we finish our earthly adventure and return to Source.

As we go through our experiences in our lives many of us start to awaken. We become conscious and aware of our true nature. We discover our purpose and our place in our reality, how we relate to it and how it relates to us. We explore our connection to the non-physical dimensions and the direct correlation between our beliefs, attitudes and the events of our lives. The more we learn and experiment the clearer it becomes that indeed, as our spiritual teachers have been telling us for thousands of years, *we are* the masters of our lives and the creators of our day to day existence, whether we know this or not. Once we are awake and conscious we become aware of our abilities and our power, and when we put into practice all we've learned we become conscious creators of our reality.

## CONSCIOUS REALITY CREATION

Human beings can live their lives either consciously or unconsciously. When we go about our days unconsciously we are on a sort of cruise control or autopilot. We do things automatically and often based on a screenplay that those who lived before us have written. The old programming is very strong, and we live our lives believing that we are lucky when life is going well and unlucky or victims of our circumstances when things don't work out in our favour. When I look back at myself throughout my life I can clearly see that I lived half my life with that mentality. I was deeply unconscious until my magic moment in Arizona (story in the introduction), after which I began to awaken and realize that I've been playing by an old, outdated screenplay all my life.

Becoming conscious is realizing that just like we can awaken in a dream we can also awaken in our life. Instead of just participating in the events of our day to day existence we can also actually observe ourselves in our environment and take control of what's happening. When we begin to create our reality consciously, life becomes a whole new and exciting ballgame. The old programming loses its hold and the new outlook on life changes everything. We no longer count on luck or any kind of power outside of ourselves to steer our life in the right direction, and we lose the victim mentality because we are now observing ourselves participating in the creation of our reality. We are not just blindly going with whatever comes up, and we can clearly see how our thoughts, beliefs and attitudes affect the outside world we are creating in every moment.

Conscious reality creation happens when you are awakened in your "play." You are aware of your part and your responsibility in the quality and circumstances of your everyday life. You use your knowledge of how your vibration and overall frequency affect you, events and other participants of your reality. You consciously manipulate energy to achieve desired results. To put it in simpler terms, conscious reality creation is the skill to make life do *your* bidding instead of you reacting to what it is seemingly randomly throwing at you.

It's important to remember that you create your reality in every moment of every day, whether you are consciously aware of it or not. When you are not awake you are creating many events and situations inadvertently, without intending to do so. Undesirable things happen and you react to them with disdain, not realizing that it was the energy of your very own mood and attitude that brought that event into your life in the first place. So to create your reality consciously is to take yourself off the cruise control, grab the steering wheel of your life with both hands and steer it exactly where you want it to go.

When you are creating your reality unconsciously you are unaware that you carry beliefs, attitudes and behaviours that came from past conditioning, trauma, and other outdated elements of your life. To be conscious is to become an observer in your reality as well as a participant. It is to recognize the source of your moods, your thoughts, and the effects of your decisions and actions on your environment and your fellow humans.

Billions of people walk the Earth unawakened and unconscious both to their abilities and their power in creating the reality they want for themselves. Because of that there is a lot of pain, misery, struggle, fear, desperation and hopelessness, due to so many feeling abandoned and powerless. When you are awake and conscious you know that you are in the driver's seat. You steer your life where you want it to go, and the feelings of vulnerability and victimhood fall away.

Another great motivator for becoming a conscious creator is to see a greater picture of your reality before you. When you are awake and conscious you refuse to look at issues from one point of view, you want to see them all! You are no longer satisfied to see a slice of a pie. You want to see the whole pie because that is the only way to get a clear picture of any situation. Since you see both or all sides of any issue you will find it difficult, if not impossible to stick up for one party in a disagreement. Now you will be aware of both sides' point of view, and see that from their own angle both of them have a valid point. So you will become a "fence sitter." You might not like the sound of that but I tell you, the top of the fence gives you a so much greater vantage point than a spot among one of the warring parties! From the top you can see the whole issue, while down there, on one side you can only see one slice of the pie. Looking at things from above is so much more beneficial for everyone involved, because from there you can clearly see any situation. You therefore have a much better chance at bringing the parties together and making peace, if that is what you are inclined to do. However, awake, aware and conscious people are very good at creating realities where there is no need for peace makers because their vibration and frequency bring high vibrational events and people into their lives, so they rarely find themselves around any kind of conflict.

What is the lesson from that? If we wish to create a world without conflicts, violence, lack, misery and powerlessness, we need to fill the planet with people who are awake, aware and conscious. People who recognize their role in their environment and know how to create a prosperous and peaceful reality both individually and en masse, using their knowledge of the effects of vibration and frequency.

*Chapter 2*

**VIBRATION AND FREQUENCY**

One of the most significant quotes from Nikola Tesla, the great inventor of the 19th century is:

*"If you want to find the secrets of the universe, think in terms of energy, frequency and vibration."*

If I want to explain that in the simplest of terms I will say that everything in the Universe is energy, and energy is always in motion. Energy in motion creates vibration, and vibration is measured in frequency. All atoms and molecules are constantly vibrating, and depending on the speed of their vibration they create a frequency. The faster the energy is vibrating the higher its frequency. Atoms and molecules vibrating together create matter: objects, organs, bodies, water, plants, planets, etc., and all those have their own unique frequency. More dense matter vibrates slower thus producing a lower frequency, while less dense matter vibrating faster creates a higher frequency.

All these Universal rules also apply to non-physical energies such as consciousness, thoughts and emotions. The thoughts we think and the emotions we feel every day are also vibrating with varying frequencies. Joy, happiness, enthusiasm and love for example are emotions creating high frequencies, while other emotions such as sadness, anger, hatred and jealousy are low vibrational, therefore creating lower frequencies.

Most of us have been taught since we were children that life out there is hard and unfair and we have to do the best we can to fit in, go with the flow, make a living and cope as well as we can. We were taught to work hard and endure while watching others struggle along with us, to help out when we can and try to be kind to each other. I didn't learn until much later in life that it doesn't have to be that way, that we actually have control over our lives because our outer reality is flexible and it is a mirror of our inner one. So if You, Dear Reader are like me, you have to unlearn a lot of old beliefs and attitudes to learn a new way of looking at your life and create the kind of reality where you can actually enjoy your time on this planet instead of just enduring it.

One of the most important and absolutely life changing piece of knowledge I received from a number of spiritual teachers throughout my journey of awakening was the concept of everyone creating every aspect of their reality. It was such a profound thought and deep inside I knew that it's true, except I had no idea what it really meant. It took me a great number of years of learning and observing my own attitudes, behaviours and their effects on my life to understand that we are indeed creating our reality in every moment, based on the frequency of our thoughts and emotions, whether we are conscious of it or not. Whatever is on the inside manifests on the outside, and once I understood that my life was never the same. And this is where the importance of the kind of frequency we are creating day after day comes in.

We are all made of conscious energy, and as such we are constantly vibrating with a certain frequency. Higher if we are happy and peaceful, lower when we are angry or tired. The reality we are creating continuously is the direct result of the frequency we are putting out. The way physical reality operates is that whatever level of frequency we send out, the Universe is answering it with events matching that frequency. If we are constantly tired and frustrated we are sending low frequency energy out there, so what we get back is more of the same.

"But, but...," you say, "we are just reacting to what happened to us during the day!"

Yes, that is true, but what happened to you during the day came about because of the kind of frequency you've been putting out! I know this is a bit of a mind bender but once you understand it it will all make sense.

We are all walking frequencies, we carry our vibration with us wherever we go. Depending on the level of our frequency we attract what we consider positive or negative experiences into our life. For example, if you are a high vibrational person with a cheerful, friendly and positive attitude, you are most likely to find yourself meeting and interacting with others of similar nature and the other way around. Like attracts like, and I've seen the proof of that all my life.

"But, but...," you say again, "I'm a nice, friendly person, and sometimes I get insulted and bullied by other people!"

Yes, it does happen, but not because the Universe is reading you wrong. It is because your frequency is the result of so much more than just your friendly personality. Let's list a few attributes here that make up the overall frequency of a person:

- Personality
- Attitude towards life
- Sense of self worth
- Belief systems
- Underlying, invisible issues
- Life circumstances

In order to understand why we attract to us the kind of events we do it is imperative that we know ourselves and that we change our perspective from that of only a participant in this earthly life to an observer as well.

As we established before, we are vibrating energy that is producing a frequency based on our thoughts, beliefs, attitudes, feelings of self worth and personality, etc. This frequency determines what kind of people and events we bring into our reality. People vibrating on a high frequency attract others and circumstances matching their output, and the same goes the other way around. So if we don't like the people around us and what's going on in our lives we have to raise our vibration, or in other words, we have to change ourselves!

The first time I heard this I was perplexed. *What does that mean, that if I don't like something or someone I have to change myself? That makes no sense! There is nothing wrong with me, it's the other people and my circumstances that are the problem! They are the ones that have to be changed!*

That is a common attitude when we look at the nature of reality through the lens of the old 3D paradigm and when we are unaware of the nature of our own being as well. However, once we become conscious of our multi-dimensional nature, understand that we are the literal creators of our reality, every aspect of it, and we learn how our frequency determines what kind of people and events we encounter, it becomes clear who is responsible for our circumstances and what we can do to make things better.

Here are some of the attributes of a person vibrating on a high frequency:

- Cheerful, positive, helpful attitude
- Friendly, peaceful demeanour
- Healthy amount of self worth, confidence
- Open-mindedness
- Glass is always half full
- Energetic, healthy body
- Love based existence

Low frequency attributes:

- Miserable, negative mindset
- Dour, unfriendly demeanour
- Low self esteem, lack of confidence
- Closed-mindedness
- Glass is always half empty
- Addictions
- Fear based existence

In order to produce the kind of frequency we wish to put out to attract desirable people and events into our lives we first must get to know ourselves. That might sound strange to some since *"Hey, I've been living with myself my whole life!"* But the truth is that a lot of people don't really know themselves because they never cared to look deep inside. Some just don't bother. They tend to run on autopilot anyway, and others don't dare to because they are afraid of what they will find if they look. Many people have deep rooted fears and traumas embedded in their past or present, and not looking too deep or at all allows them to cope with their own emotions and generally with life better. However, if we want to become conscious creators of our reality we cannot leave anything lurking beneath our conscious awareness, because all those "invisibles" are affecting our attitudes, beliefs and behaviours, therefore they are part of our overall frequency.

Here are some of the "invisibles" that affect people even if they are not consciously aware of them:

- Trauma suffered in childhood or as an adult (physical, mental, emotional abuse)
- Past conditioning
- Previous incarnational experiences

*"Knowing ourselves is the beginning of all wisdom",*
Aristotle

Long before our present civilization the ancient philosophers already understood the importance of looking into the deepest part of our being and learning all that we can about ourselves. Looking deep enough to see all that is visible and what is hidden is the key to finding the reasons for attitudes and behavioural patterns we display, those that directly affect our vibration and therefore our overall frequency. Once we discover the hidden content of our psyche and process what we find inside we can clear it, let it go, and we will not only know ourselves better but feel much lighter as our frequency becomes higher. I will talk about different methods of accomplishing this task later in the book.

I am convinced that low vibrational personality traits and attitudes are the culprits of most of the "bad luck," unfortunate events and low quality existence experienced by many throughout their lives. Low frequency output brings low frequency results, that is why it is so important to be aware of our own thoughts, beliefs and attitudes that create our behaviours and our reality.

Low vibrational attitudes can come from not only ourselves but other sources as well, and if we accept and integrate them into our belief system they will have a negative effect on our frequency, therefore bringing undesirable outcomes for us. For example, a person who's never had a romantic interaction with anyone can read many negative stories about others' encounters, and without any personal experience whatsoever can decide that "a*ll men are pigs*" or "w*omen just want men with money*." When people radiate that kind of attitude what can the Universe do but match it, frequency for frequency, so it is no surprise if they end up meeting exactly those type of romantic partners. The more negative experiences they encounter in their search of "the right one" brought on by their own beliefs, the more it will seem like they were right in their original assessment. This is a vicious cycle brought on by beliefs created unconsciously, and can only be stopped by consciously examining and recognizing the attitude, the belief it is based on, and the source of that belief. Once we know where the belief came from it can be corrected. That approach works with all beliefs and attitudes.

*Chapter 3*

**CREATING A HIGH VIBRATIONAL REALITY**

If you desire to create a high frequency life full of high vibrational people and events, you need to offer high frequency attitudes that the Universe can match. I'm going to talk about a number of ways to raise your vibration when it is low, and how to maintain it once it reaches high.

Low vibrational thoughts, emotions, attitudes and behaviours are easy to recognize, they are what we refer to as "negative." They include:

- misery
- hatred
- malevolence
- judgement
- complaining
- victim mentality
- fear
- jealousy
- violence

The majority of people go through life spending a great deal of their time observing and reading about others, criticizing their choices and actions, making judgements, complaining about their own misfortunes and focusing on so called negative events happening in the world. The result of displaying all of these attitudes and actions on a regular basis is that people operate on a low vibration, and therefore keep producing a low overall frequency that the Universe will match. These individuals tend to experience a drama filled, often turbulent everyday life with a lot of ups and downs, and all of that keeps the low vibrations going. Humanity has been spinning with this low vibrational wheel individually and en masse for thousands of years, creating wars, lack, fear, inequality and a generally miserable existence for itself.

To get out of this wheel there are several steps we have to take, both individually and en masse. This starts with becoming conscious of our thoughts, emotions, words and behaviours.

1. Instead of running on autopilot you must become aware of the thoughts that enter your mind because that is where everything starts. You have to recognize the low vibrational thoughts and send them away, replacing them with high vibrational ones, preferably before expressing them.

2. Examine your thoughts and beliefs. When you take a look at the contents of your mind you might be surprised

by all the stuff you find. A lot of them came from your childhood, social conditioning, religious education, etc. You need to take a close look at them and sort them out.

3. Choose what you say consciously. Why? Because words have power. Our ancestors knew this but we have forgotten, and now it is time we remembered. As we have established earlier, everything is energy. Everything is also consciousness, and consciousness is always aware and listening. What we refer to as Universe or Source or All That Is is all consciousness, and it is always ready to answer the instructions coming from us in the form of our frequency and that includes words. Once you have mastered sorting out your thoughts and watching what you allow out of your mouth, you just have to keep practising doing it all the time until it becomes second nature.

I was in my mid thirties when I first became consciously aware of the words coming out of my mouth. My children were small, and one day after playing outside they came into the house covered in mud, grass and god knows what else. I threw up my hands in indignation and started complaining about how I'm going to have to wash their clothes now, and suddenly I began to hear my words. Not just hear them, but HEAR them with full awareness. I was startled out of my tirade because the things I was saying now didn't make any sense. Why would it matter that my children's clothes were muddy? Of course they would be, the boys were playing outside. So what if I have to do a load of laundry? The washer and dryer will do it, my involvement will take only a few minutes so what am I freaking out for?

It took me a few moments to realize that I was actually speaking my parents' and grandparents' words. Those thoughts that I just verbalized originated from decades ago, from a time when washing machines were either non-existent in my family or they had one already, but living in tiny apartments doing laundry was still a lot of hassle. I've often heard those words directed at me as a child, coming from my parents, grandparents and even a great grand-parent, and they took up permanent residence in my subconscious. Now, as I found myself in the appropriate situation in the present, those long stored words broke free from their hidey-hole and flew out of my mouth un-checked.

This event was a turning point in my life, because it was as if the fog cleared and now I was finally awake and aware. I could understand the thoughts in my head and consciously hear everything that I said out loud. It was a rather disconcerting experience at first but I got used to it fairly quickly, especially because of the sense of awareness it brought. It felt very much like freedom, like new opportunities, like looking at the world with a new set of eyes. This was the moment when the old programming started to lose its hold, and it was also an excellent first step on my journey of awakening.

Once you start living your life consciously with awareness of the contents of your mind and their direct effect on your reality, life as you know it will change forever. You will no longer be surprised and disappointed by what it "throws at you," or expect some outside force to solve your problems for you. You will be fully aware that the people and the events you encounter are those that *you* attracted to yourself with *your* frequency.

There are of course always exceptions because existence in physical reality is rarely so simple and straightforward. We are multidimensional beings living in a multiverse dealing with karma, low dimensional entities, contracts we made before we were born, and most importantly, the amnesia that is caused by the extremely dense nature of the third dimensional reality we were born into. We set a life purpose and challenges for ourselves for this Earth experience and we keep them coming until we "get it." These challenges can cause us difficulties, but we are slowly losing them as we keep raising our vibration and are slowly ascending into higher frequencies, awakening to our true nature. That is why it is in our very best interest to understand how creating our reality works, including the importance of vibration, frequency, intent, focus, and staying in the present. I will speak about those as well later in the book. But for now, please remember:

*FREQUENCY IS EVERYTHING!*

Getting rid of low vibrational thoughts, emotions and attitudes takes intent, time, patience, self discipline and practice, but it is a truly worthwhile undertaking.

Here are a few practical tips you can use during your journey:

The DON'Ts:

- When you have a negative experience don't dwell on it. Acknowledge that it happened, the feelings it produced, and walk away from it. Do not tell everyone who is willing to listen and keep recounting the event. Acknowledge and move on.

- When someone pushes in front of you in a line, cuts you off when you drive or makes a rude remark towards you, don't react with anger and frustration. Understand that the other person may have had a bad day, is in a rush, or could be dealing with emotional, mental and other issues in their life. Their problem is not you, it is themselves. If the situation is your fault for any reason then apologize and move on. When you react to anger with anger the low vibe energy envelops and drains both of you.

- Don't try to convince anyone of anything. Your beliefs and opinions are yours, and theirs are theirs. You will only create arguments that will put all parties of the disagreement into a low vibration.

- Don't complain.

- Don't hold grudges. If you get into an argument try not to stay in it for too long, and once it's over let it all go. Holding a grudge is not going to hurt your opponent, it will hurt *You* by keeping you in a low vibration. If you hold on to your anger and resentment long enough, the constant low vibrational energy tends to manifest itself in forms of illnesses.

- Don't compare yourself to anyone, for every person on this planet is different. They came in for different reasons with different life plans, purposes, contracts and challenges. Their journey is theirs, and yours is yours.

- Don't worry. As they say, worrying is praying for something you don't want. Trust me, it's true. I'm speaking from experience.

The DOs:

- If you have a disagreement with someone keep your cool. If it is no longer possible and the talk becomes an argument, end it. Politely walk away and get back to it when you are in a peaceful state, or the best is to end it altogether.

- Meditate. I cannot tell you how important learning to keep your mind clear is. It settles and relaxes you, keeps you in the present and strengthens your awareness of your connection to your non-physical, multidimensional selves.

- When you come home tired and frazzled from a busy workday take time for yourself and relax. Even 10 minutes can make a difference. On the couch or the bed, in the bath, wherever you have the chance. When you are tired it is hard to keep your vibes up, and grumpiness tends to spread.

- Mind your own business. Everyone has a life with challenges and issues. Involving yourself into others' negative stories will keep you in low vibration as well.

- Stay away from gossip. It is a harmful activity for all parties involved.

- Tame your ego. If not checked, your ego can keep you in a continuous low vibration. There will be more details on this in a later chapter.

- Forgive. You may have been mistreated, hurt, abused, made to feel less than what you are in the past, and if you carry the anger and resentment with you, you will hurt yourself in the present. Those emotions carry a lot of negative energy and they have to be released. Forgiveness clears a great deal of low vibrational energy out of your body.

- Limit your News time. People spend a lot of time reading and watching the news of the world that is full of low vibrational information. If you want to stay informed read, acknowledge and move on. Or just stay away from the news media altogether.

- Choose high vibrational entertainment. Enjoy books, movies and music with cheerful, uplifting and empowering messages.

- Do some form of exercise. It doesn't have to be in the gym or the yoga studio, it could be just something you do at home. Walking or jumping up the stairs, skipping a rope, dancing and going for a hike outside are all excellent activities that will fill you with high vibrational energy.

- Eat less dense foods. Lighter foods are easier to digest and they have a higher vibration. It has been proven that food grown in the sun brings light energy into the body.

- Spend time in nature. When you walk in the forest or watch and listen to the waves on a beach, you can tell that you are in a high vibrational environment by the way it makes you feel.

- Let go of relationships that no longer serve you and are not for your highest good. Toxicity among friends and family keeps millions of people in low vibration.

- Find something to do that makes you feel good every day. Read a few pages of a good book, take a walk, listen to some music, have a cup of tea. The most ordinary things that put a smile on your face will make a big difference.

- Surround yourself with people who support you. By that I don't mean only people who think just like you, although you need a couple of those as well. It's great to have your tribe around you. But I was also talking about people who might not think like you at all, but they love you and respect your beliefs whatever they may be. They are there for you to help you succeed.

- Set an example. Live your life on the highest vibration you can and watch people take notice. As we are all conscious energy we affect those around us, spreading our frequency wherever we go whether consciously or unconsciously. When you walk around carrying a high frequency it will impact everyone you meet, and it can be a life changer for those you interact with.

I have learned all of these methods during my journey of awakening, used every single one of them, and I can vouch for their effectiveness. Following and practising them took time, patience, dedication and self discipline, and it was well worth it. After a few years of work on my thoughts, beliefs and attitudes I have reached a point where I had no major issues in my life. No drama, no ups and downs that used to be the norm in both my private and professional life. The Universe keeps matching the level of frequency I'm putting out just as it has always done, except now instead of driving blind I'm holding the steering wheel with both eyes open.

*Chapter 4*

# THE TOOLS OF CONSCIOUS REALITY CREATION

There are a number of useful tools available to us to help with creating a desirable and high vibrational existence for ourselves, and as a consequence, each other. When we are in peace and fulfilled our frequency positively affects others, raising their frequency as well. This way we are creating a higher vibrational mass reality, which is the very reason why the lightworkers are here. We came to assist in humanity's ascension to higher dimensions, by spreading our frequencies wherever we go.

Here is a list of some of the most important tools of creating and maintaining our high frequency vibration, and as a result, our desirable reality.

- Intent
- Beliefs
- Focus
- Visualization
- Manifestation

- Using the Innate
- Meditation
- Dropping Expectations
- Acceptance
- Living in the present
- Affirmations

## INTENT

I put *Intent* on top because that's where it all starts. It is a powerful reality creation tool because this is the one that gets things going. When you consciously set an intention the Universe knows you mean it, and it moves to give you what you need to turn that intent into reality. Whether you are creating small or bigger events, a strong intent combined with focus, visualization and/or other tools can give you excellent results.

To give you a few examples I will use events from my own experiences to show you how setting an intent can bring what we desire into reality at the end of this book. For now I will say that it can be as simple as saying:

*"It is my intent to wake up well rested and fresh tomorrow morning, arrive safely wherever I go, and have a productive, successful day at work."*

Or how about this one:

*"It is my intent to be open only to positive thoughts and suggestions throughout my days."*

Both of these are very helpful, for they will raise you into a higher vibrational state and keep you there as long as you stay conscious of your intent and pay attention to your thoughts.

As for bigger events, you can set your intent to buy your dream home, write your first book, meet friends or romantic partners, start a business, create a new job, go on a much desired trip to your dream destination, and the list goes on forever. As they say, you can accomplish anything if you set your mind to it, and I can vouch for that. Once you set the intent the Universe WILL create a pathway for you to get there, you just have to follow the signs and take the opportunities when they arise. I used intent to create outcomes for myself long before I became awake and aware. I did it unconsciously, without knowing what I was instinctively doing. Now imagine setting your intent to create your reality consciously and fully aware of your power to make your dreams come true!

## BELIEFS

There is no other element that is as singularly important in creating our reality as our belief system. Our personal and mass beliefs determine the very nature of our experiences; they can make us or break us. That is why we'd better be sure we know ourselves and the full content of our beliefs about anything and everything.

A person who is not aware and conscious of all their personal beliefs will have more difficulties in reaching their goals and creating their desired outcome, because by having hidden limiting and negative beliefs they sabotage themselves. Our beliefs are a part of our frequency, therefore they create the environment, events and the people we encounter every day. Positive beliefs being high vibrational bring favourable experiences, while negative ones being low vibrational, the opposite.

People who are unconscious of their thoughts and beliefs can set an intent, focus, visualize and use all the available tools to reach their goal, and still find that all of that is not working because their beliefs contradict their words. A good example of that is someone who is dreaming of a prosperous and happy life, but carries an underlying belief of being weak, unlucky and undeserving. Or those looking for a loving partner in a relationship but holding negative beliefs about the other sex, people and dating in general, or about themselves as partners. Another good example is the one who has all the intentions of losing weight, yet makes jokes about gaining a pound every time they look at a piece of cake. Or the person who believes that one must work hard for their money, yet complains about the hardship of making a living.

The Universe is always listening, or to be more precise, you are broadcasting your frequency all the time! Your frequency contains all your thoughts, beliefs, desires, attitudes, etc. You can't intend one thing, think and believe another, and expect the Universe to give you what you are asking for.

Most people in the world go about their lives unconsciously, without being aware of all the things about themselves that affect their vibration and overall frequency. They live their life unaware, unfocused, with random events and lots of drama surrounding them. They end up believing that life and the world are a hot mess that one must survive and requires a great deal of hard work and luck to succeed in. Those who are awake and conscious know that nothing is further from the truth. We are the creators of our reality, with the power of both our own multidimensional being and the Universe at our back.

## FOCUS

As we established at the beginning of this book, everything is consciousness and energy: people, places, objects, thoughts, emotions, all of it. We are all individualized consciousnesses, vibrating energy that is affecting everything around us. When we focus our consciousness on something we give it energy, and in time bring it into our reality. The longer we focus on it the longer we will see or experience it. When individual consciousnesses work together and focus on the same thing they create a mass consciousness focus that is a lot more powerful, and can bring on changes faster or keep something in existence longer.

This phenomenon is fairly easy to see in our everyday life if we pay attention to it. When we focus on something (be it good or bad) we give it power and keep it up front and centre. Something pops up, some issue with someone or something. It inconveniences us so we talk about it, we dwell on it, we complain about it. It persists. It refuses to go away so we complain and dwell some more, not realizing that by keeping our focus on it we keep it alive, in our face, because we are continuously giving it energy. It is the same with what we consider the good things. The more we concentrate on something the faster we bring it into our reality, and the longer we keep it there.

It is very important to be aware of the power of our focus because if we use it wrong we will be creating all kinds of things that we don't want, alongside of the things we do. A lot of people make this mistake and are surprised when things don't go their way.

The Universe is constantly reading you, therefore you have to be pretty clear about what you are focusing on. Whatever it is, it's part of your vibration that you broadcast to the energy field, so keep an eye on where your attention is. For example, if you keep being worried about burglars breaking into your home and can't stop dwelling on how they are everywhere and your house may be hit next, you might find yourself having to face the experience. Your vibration says 'burglars,' 'I don't feel safe,' so the Universe will match that by sending you the very thing you are focusing on. The more you are afraid of something the longer you keep it in your focus, therefore the bigger chance you have to encounter it. So if not applied properly, your focus can bring you things you'd rather not have. That is why you have to be consciously aware of what you are giving your attention to at all times.

A good example of this comes from my own experience. Before our final exams at high school we all had to study a number of theses in a number of subjects. During the oral exams we drew the title of a thesis out of a box, randomly, in every subject. We had to recite all we recalled about them and thus we got graded. I was a good student and studied a lot for this exam, especially since the resulting grade affected our future prospects in education and employment. I learned most of the theses well, except for one or two that I thought I could "wing it" if I had to. There was a lot to learn after all. We did a lot of cramming and only so much can fit in one's head, right?

The night before and the morning of the exam I kept saying: "I'm ready to draw any thesis but the one titled 'The Ancient Greek Voting System.' Not the Greek voting! I know everything else!"

You can probably guess which one I drew. Out of the dozens of theses I could have chosen I ended up with the one I absolutely did not want. Bad luck? God hates me? No. I drew that one because it was the one I focused on. On top of that, being all nervous about the exam I gave it a lot of frantic energy, and that pretty much invited that thesis to end up being the one I had to face.

A number of authors have talked about focusing on what you want to see and cited this next example before, but it bears repeating: if you are a pacifist marching and protesting on the streets, your banner must say 'WE WANT PEACE!' not 'No more war!' When you talk about how you hate war your frequency is 'war' and 'hate,' and it will not bring you peace. If peace is what you want, it is peace you have to focus on. That has to be your frequency that you broadcast to the Universe.

The lesson to learn here? If you hate violence focus on gentleness. If you dislike enmity focus on friendship, and if you don't want to see hate in the world and in your personal life focus on love.

## VISUALIZATION

One of the greatest tools of consciously creating our reality is visualization. It can be used for many things like conflict resolution, clearing old issues, sending energy, healing and manifesting, just to name a few I have experience with. Combining it with any or all of the other methods makes it a powerful assistant in creating a desired outcome. I have used it for most of the above mentioned reasons with excellent results. Here are a few examples:

Conflict resolution

If you have a person in your life you don't get along with, you can change the situation with the following visualization technique. First, set the intent to have a good relationship with the person. If you state it out loud to yourself that can add to its power. Then, as you go about your day visualize yourself expressing positive attitudes and friendly gestures towards the person. Have an imaginary conversation with them, telling them that you want to have a great relationship. You forgive all the previous behaviours, apologize for your own, and now it's time to get along and work well together. After that you just keep visualizing friendly encounters between the two of you, such as a smile, a hug, etc.

Now, if you are comfortable with confrontations and prefer solving your problems straight and direct, you can have this conversation with the one you don't get along with out loud. However, if you are like me and don't like confrontations this is a good way to go. This approach takes time and effort but it works.

Clearing old issues

When discussing the relevance of the level of frequency we are vibrating with, I talked about the many hidden or not so hidden issues people are storing both in their conscious awareness and subconscious. Regardless of whether these past traumas, regrets, guilt, old beliefs, grudges, resentments and the like are on the surface or deeply hidden, they must be dealt with. Holding on to them is keeping many people in low vibration, depressed, manifesting bad relationships, difficult circumstances, and a great number of illnesses. It is therefore imperative that these issues are brought to the surface, faced, acknowledged, forgiven and released. If the issues are deep within, professional help might be needed to bring them to the surface, and once they are in the open we can do the work to release them ourselves.

Everyone, I dare say, without exception, throughout their lifetime accumulates issues that affect their emotions, beliefs, attitudes and behaviours, and therefore their level of vibration. Until we deal with those issues, not just our everyday existence but our entire worldview remain continuously coloured by those unresolved issues we are carrying around with us. Therefore the sooner we clear them the better.

There are a number of ways we can do the clearing; with the help of a professional, with a friend, by ourselves, or the combination of those. If you choose to do clearing with a trusted friend make sure this is a high vibrational person who knows what his/her task is in the process. They are there to give you the opportunity to freely talk about whatever is weighing you down. Their purpose is to calmly listen without any judgement, opinion or taking sides. They will be absolutely no use to you if for example you talk about a bad relationship you are or have been in and they go "Oh that bastard!" or "You really shouldn't have done that!" Their task is to be the witness to your catharsis and encourage you to release your burden, not to make judgements. Once the issue has been acknowledged it is time to forgive the perpetrator of your hardship and suffering, and/or yourself. You must forgive in order to release the energy of the emotion.

There are many who have suffered great traumas and hardships by others who will find it very difficult to forgive. They will insist that they can't because the offence was too horrible and their hurt is too deep, but they must forgive if they want to release the negative energy of their resentment and move on with their life. If they can't forgive they will keep carrying their issues around that will negatively affect their vibration, their health, and therefore their reality.

When I was doing my clearing I had no one around me I trusted to help me with it. Being an immigrant all my friends were living overseas, and this was before Skype and Messenger came into worldwide use so I had to do it all by myself. I found visualization the perfect tool for this task.

To do release work I visualized imaginary conversations between me and the person(s) who caused my issues. In my mind I told them how much they hurt me, how difficult it was to carry that hurt around and that I was ready to let it all go. I told them I forgive them for their words and actions and harbour no ill will towards them. I visualized them being remorseful and contrite, and apologizing for the hurt they caused me. I also told myself that I understand and forgive any part I, myself might have played in those events. At the end I imagined myself smiling at those I was speaking to and gave their hand a squeeze or hugged them. There were tears and emotional pain while I was doing this, but the release came with a sense of relief. Not right away, but gradually I felt lighter and lighter, and at one point I was able to look at the released issues and people objectively, without emotion. That's when I knew that I was successful.

Another excellent way of doing all this for people whom are not open to talking about their issues and have trouble visualizing is journaling. You can write down all your anger, hurts and resentment into a notebook, and by doing that you unload your inner burden and record words of understanding and forgiveness onto the pages. It will free you from the heavy emotional baggage you've been carrying around for a long time. What was inside you all this time will now be out; out of your heart, out of your mind and out of your system. Your burden will be released, the energy blocks from your chakras cleaned out, so your vibration can now be raised.

Clearing past trauma can be quite difficult. The deeper the wound the harder it is to face it. It helps if you remember that by mistreating you these people were most likely playing out their part of a contract both or more of you made. And once the release work is done the contract will be fulfilled and those issues will no longer drag you down. They will no longer affect your beliefs, attitudes and behaviours, and will not be obstacles to raising your vibration and therefore your frequency.

Healing and sending energy

A great number of people use visualization for healing and sending energy to others. A lot of us have been participating in individual and mass meditations for a cause, Reiki, quantum healing and other modalities. All of these involve moving and transferring energy with the help of visualization. As always, there is strength in numbers, so when a large number of people are visualizing and focusing on a single purpose it has a powerful effect.

I have learned from others and developed a few self healing methods on my own, using visualization alone. Try these and see if they work for you:

The Balloon method:
When I have a headache I imagine a white balloon with the word 'HEADACHE' written on it. This balloon rises from my head up into the air, goes higher and higher, and then with a loud "POP!" it bursts and its pieces slowly fall to the ground. I sweep them onto a dustpan with a brush or a broom and dump them into a garbage bin. After this visualization I turn my attention away to something else. In 10-15 minutes the headache is usually gone.

The Ball method:
When I get the hiccups I know it's because my yellow energy centre goes out of whack, so I visualize a yellow ball spinning clockwise for about 20-30 seconds. Then I move my attention away from the hiccups, and either right away or soon after they are gone. The yellow ball represents my solar plexus chakra, and by mentally spinning it I clear it. This method is used by other members of my family as well, and they practice it with great success.

The Healing Station method:
I visualize a place out in nature that I use for self healing. It's a small wooden hut on a tiny island on a lake. At the head of the wooden bridge that takes me across there is a sign that says 'HEALING STATION.' From the shore I walk across the bridge, approach the hut and see a beautiful, emerald green healing light coming from the ceiling. I step inside and stand underneath the light, feeling

it envelop and permeate my body, and I remain there for a while, enjoying the slight fizzing and buzzing sensations all over me. After a while the light disappears, I bow and say "thank you!" and leave the hut, walking back across the bridge to the shore.

These self healing methods can all be adapted to your own individual taste. You can create a great healing station for yourself made out of anything, wood, marble or glass, it can be a building, a place or whatever you can visualize for yourself. The only rules are the ones you set. Any way you imagine it, it will work for you if you believe it will.

When it comes to the subject of healing I would like to shortly mention the role of our energy centres, the Chakras. There is a vast volume of material out there to teach us what they are and how they work so I won't go into great details about them. I will just say that the purpose of the chakras is to move consciousness and energy in and out of the human body. As we encounter and go through energies of feelings, emotions and events throughout our life we process them, they go through these spinning energy centres and leave the body. That is, unless we are holding on to issues, grudges, resentments and negative beliefs. Those low vibrational energies clog the system. A healthy chakra system is clear of blockages with the energy centres spinning freely, so it can receive, filter, transmute and release energies all the time.

There are many kinds of spiritual/quantum healing modalities that are available to help bring you relief from aches, pains, physical and non-physical health problems. However, if you don't process, clear and release your personal emotional, mental and other issues that keep blocking your energy centres, your health problems will return.

The human body is designed to be healthy and self correcting, but it can't heal itself if the energy centres are constantly blocked by negative energy. Clearing/releasing is an important task that cannot be neglected until you raise your frequency high enough that you no longer create new issues, therefore new blockages.

## MANIFESTATION

Every person is creating their life in every moment by manifesting events, people and circumstances based on their own vibration. This is done either consciously or not. Unconscious creators (again, this is most people in the world) bring all sorts of undesired elements into their life by not paying attention to their beliefs, attitudes and what they are focusing on. Before I became aware of my power to consciously create what I wanted I also manifested a good number of messy events for myself, some of which affected me short term, others for many years to come. I'd like to mention two events that "happened to me" that clearly shows the 'cause and effect' dynamics of manifestation.

When my older son was in fifth grade I had a parent-teacher meeting scheduled for one morning to discuss his progress in his studies. I was not looking forward to this, for both me and my son nursed a great dislike for this particular teacher. Previous discussions with her left me feeling frustrated, so the idea of having another fruitless talk with her filled me with a certain level of anxiety. The night before the meeting I was tossing and turning in my bed, and my first thought the moment I woke up in the morning was *"Oh god, I don't want to do this!"* On top of that I heard the sound of pouring rain through the window, and the level of my uneasiness went up a few notches.

My husband took the car to work so I had no transportation which usually wasn't a problem, for the school was a mere 10-15 minutes walk away and we made the trip on foot many times before. But because of the pouring rain the task of walking to the meeting seemed rather daunting. So I really didn't want to go but could not think of a reasonable excuse to get out of it, no matter how feverishly I was searching my mind for one. Not having found a good enough reason to stay home I decided to just get up and get on with it. Except that I couldn't, because the moment I moved to get out of bed I suffered an intensely painful attack of sciatica, something that never happened to me before. I remained bed bound for hours, for I could not move from the pain in the back of my right thigh, so I had to call the school and leave a message for the teacher that I would not be able to attend our meeting.

When my husband came home from work he helped me into the car and we went to the clinic to see a doctor. As I was sitting in the waiting room wondering why all this happened today, it dawned on me that I was the one who created this event to stop myself from having to face my son's teacher. It was a rather startling realization, but I had no doubt that my feelings about this were right. Further proof for this is that I have not had another one of these attacks ever since, so I'm quite sure in my assessment of my part in this event.

The second time I created an undesirable event where I recognized my responsibility in its manifestation was at my workplace. I worked at a mostly automated, fast paced bakery, where one thing we had to do by hand was putting plastic trays on a conveyor line. It was hard work and one had to be pretty fast to keep up with the line, but I was used to it and didn't mind, I considered it my daily exercise. What I did mind though was that Thanksgiving Monday was coming up and I was scheduled to work on that day. I felt quite resentful for that because my son was coming home from college for the holiday and I planned to roast a turkey and celebrate together with my family, not toil away in the factory like I did on so many occasions before. So once I saw my work schedule I got pretty worked up over it, and carried the feeling of resentment and pissiness with me all over the factory.

As I was working in the tray room, putting the trays on the line, I conducted an emotional and frustrated monologue in my head, internally complaining about the unfairness of having to work on a holiday when I just wanted to be with my family. Is that so much to ask?!

The next moment there was a sharp pain in my knee and my right leg went out from under me. Someone came and took over my job, my husband came to pick me up and drove me to the hospital. It turned out I twisted my knee and sprained a ligament. I was instructed to stay off the leg for a couple of days.

As we were driving home, the recognition of the part I played in this event came to me with absolute clarity. I could clearly see how my mood and angry thoughts created this situation. I have to say though that I wasn't too sad about what happened, for the price of a bit of pain, inconvenience and loss of a few hours worth of wages I got myself a free Thanksgiving holiday!

Through these two memorable and eye opening events I have learned how we manifest undesirable things when we are not conscious of our thoughts and actions. These days I keep a close eye on mine, and I'm happy to say I have not manifested that kind of a mess ever since.

To consciously create - or manifest - desired elements of our reality, the more of the available tools we use the better. Together they complement each other and each adds a step to the manifestation process.

Here are the steps I use for conscious manifesting:

1. Setting the intent
2. Focusing on my goal
3. Verbalizing my affirmations
4. Visualizing positive results
5. Watching for signs, nudges and opportunities arising
6. Keeping a positive, high vibe attitude throughout the process
7. Once my goal is achieved, expressing my gratitude to the Universe

Again, in order to manifest what you desire you first have to set an intent. Your intent to create something is the "Listen up!" to the Universe. I tend to verbalize mine because I believe that saying it out loud gives it more power. Once you set your intent and verbalize it spend time visualizing what you want to accomplish, and feel the emotions that you know will come with your success.

Let's say you are looking for a new home. State your intent and in your mind's eye picture yourself finding it. Imagine the excitement of it, how happy you will be, how great it will be to paint it, furnish it, decorate it and make it your own. Make sure you bring as much emotion into the visualization as you can because it adds more energy to it. Try not to be too specific though. Do not create a rigid image of a house that must be exactly the way you imagined because with set expectations you can limit yourself. I will talk about that in greater detail later in the book.

If you have trouble visualizing what you wish to manifest, an excellent tool you can use is a vision board. It can be made using photos, drawings, newspaper clippings, whatever you find that can express what you would like to create and stir up an excited energy within you.

Along with visualization you can also use affirmations, such as *"I will find my dream house and love my new home because it will suit my needs very well!"*

Listen to your gut feelings: what feels right and what doesn't, should you take this agent or that. Your inner voice will guide you, you just have to be open and listen. Use your focus to hone in on what you want by looking at real estate listings, agents, home decoration ideas and moving companies. Remember to concentrate on the things you want and not the ones you don't. Do not read real estate and moving company horror stories. I know there are tons out there. Believe me, that's not where you want your attention to be. To successfully manifest your desires you need to be clear, steady, full of positive intentions and excited energy, and free of preconceived notions, judgements and expectations.

## USING THE INNATE

The innate is an inner sense, a knowing, an instinct, an intuition, an inner compass, a sixth sense that comes from our subconscious. It is a silent guide that's with us throughout our journey of life in the physical, often nudging us towards our goals whether we acknowledge its existence or not. It is the nagging feeling, the thought in the back of our mind that won't leave us alone. It is the sensation that we should be going this way instead of that. This is our inner guide that knows the intent we set and the reality we want to create. Its purpose among other things is to help us along by nudging us in the right direction, to get our attention when we need to be alert, and warn us when we encounter a questionable situation.

Everybody has experiences with their innate throughout their life. People usually describe it as a feeling that something is not right, or a persistent thought that won't go away, a knowing, or "the little voice in my head." It is our inner guide giving us a heads up, letting us know that we need to pay attention to something. I have felt this sensation many times in my life and sometimes followed its guidance. Other times I allowed logic to take me in a different direction. I cannot tell you how many times I ended up wishing that I had listened to my "heart" instead of my brain.

Our innate is an important part of our multi-dimensional makeup that's continuously working to assist us. It is a worthwhile effort to train ourselves to be consciously aware of it and pay attention to it. I could have avoided a number of pitfalls throughout my life had I paid more attention to the nagging sensations, gut feelings and the little voice in my head, taken them seriously and taken their advice.

How does the innate know which way we should go? Since it is a multidimensional part of our being, the innate is not bound by the rules of linearity. It can "see" where we are, where we are heading and what kind of probabilities we can choose from. It sees what kind of obstacles are in our way and how to get around them.

Many people use their innate to their advantage. However, many more don't trust their inner voice and when they subconsciously receive heads ups or nudges, using the logical mind they talk themselves out of any actions their inner guide suggests.

The innate is always working to steer us towards our highest good, so I highly recommend that you take advantage of its benevolent guidance. Be conscious and aware, and pay attention to your gut feelings, nudges and persistent thoughts. They will steer you towards your goals even though it may not seem so at times. Remember, the innate is multidimensional and it can see the things you don't. If you allow it, it will lead you wherever you want to go. It is your silent helper. Make good use of it!

## MEDITATION

Meditation was one of the hardest things for me to learn because my mind was always so active with daydreams, opinions, inner commentaries and music. It was quite a challenge to silence them all. Once mastering the quieting of the mind though I could see the many advantages it brought, like getting to know the greater multidimensional *Me*, my non-physical existence I never before knew about.

There are psychics who are naturally gifted and don't need to get into a meditative state in order to communicate with the non-physical. The majority of people have to work at it though, experiment with it and practice until they develop their method of accessing the quantum field or the Akashic records. Those who learn to do it are able to catch glimpses of other realities, "past" lives and experiment with projections of consciousness, remote viewing, etc. I very much enjoyed my trips to the "other side" while meditating, and kept a diary about my psychic adventures.

How to meditate? When I was starting out I searched for ways to learn different methods of meditation and found a great number of them that taught to silence the mind, but which one to choose? At the end of the day it came down to just taking deep breaths and trying my best to think of nothing.

At first I could go only for a few seconds without a thought intruding, but with practice I improved very fast. I learned to quiet my mind and push away any uninvited thoughts that popped into my head. Then, since the Universe knew what I was up to, my third eye started to open and the visions and other forms of psychic adventures began.

Here are a few examples of how I used to access the quantum field through meditation:

This is another visualization, similar to the one I created for healing. I lay down, take several deep breaths while verbalizing my intent to access the quantum field. I visualize myself walking in a beautiful green forest on a dirt path, with a creek running over rocks on my right. I walk to the edge of the creek, squat down, splash some water on my face to refresh myself and walk on. I reach a wooden bridge where I see a white sign on a wooden pole saying 'COMMUNICATION STATION' with purple-pink-violet colouring. I cross the creek by walking over the bridge, and on the other side there is an open sided small wooden hut with another sign, the same as the one at the bridge. As I walk into the hut I notice a column of purple-pink-violet light coming from the ceiling. I step under the light, feel it envelop me, and the top of my head begins to get fizzy and bubbly. As I visualize this, first I see a pink/violet light swirling in my mind's eye, then I start getting images, still pictures and those that are video-like. Some are in colour, others black and white. They last about 3-10 seconds each.

A fairly easy way to get into a meditative state where visions can appear is to learn to wake up slowly. There is a certain zone between being asleep and awake where we are not asleep anymore but our consciousness is still tuned into the quantum field. In this drowsy state I used to be able to still access other realities while being aware of my body and my surroundings, right until I fully woke up and opened my eyes. In this in-between state I have had projections of consciousness where I found myself looking into a room with furniture, a duffle bag on the floor and a digital alarm clock with glowing green numbers. At another time I saw a zoomed in image of a stone carving that kept coming closer and closer. Sometimes it seemed like I was looking at these images through a tube.

One day I fell into one of those almost-asleep-but-not-quite states during a long car trip. I was aware of the car's movements and heard the music playing, but I was too sleepy to open my eyes. So I found myself in an altered state of consciousness where I was looking at an image very much like a Google map. I wish I had time to take a closer look and find out which city's map I was looking at, but there wasn't enough time for that. All of these events lasted no more that 15 seconds, and once I fully awakened I wrote them down into my ESP diary.

Another great way to get a peek into other realities, past lives and probable futures is training yourself to remember your dreams. I have glimpsed probable futures that became reality several times, once after two weeks and another time after 4 years. How did I know? I trained myself to not just remember but also record my dreams in a diary sitting on my bedside table. One day at work I found myself in a situation that seemed very familiar to me and I had a strong feeling of déjà vu. After I got home I checked my diaries and lo and behold, there it was, the event that I experienced that day written down 4 years before. So whenever you feel like *"Hey, I've been here or this happened to me before,"* you bet that you've encountered that situation in your dream or in a vision before, you just don't remember.

Whether you are aware of it or not, you are and always have been connected to your multi-dimensional selves and the Universe. By meditating regularly you consciously maintain your connection to the non-physical. I encourage you to work on silencing your mind and relaxing your body. With the busy lifestyle of modern everyday existence it is often not easy to find time for meditation, but I strongly urge you to do so. Our connection to our inner being is of the outmost importance if we want to learn who and what we really are, and how to consciously and successfully navigate our life.

When I started awakening I was a busy working mother of two young children. I worked a late afternoon shift, getting to bed at 2-3 o'clock in the morning and getting up at 8 to get the boys ready and send them to school. As soon as they were out the door I had my own breakfast, cleaned up the kitchen and headed upstairs for a meditation session.

I set the alarm for one hour in case I fell asleep during meditation, which occasionally happened due to my constant sleep deprived state. Once the alarm went off I recorded my experiences in my ESP diary, then it was time to do my shopping or run other errands, make dinner for the family for the evening and then go to work. It was an incredibly busy and exhausting time of my life, but I always made time for my daily meditation because I knew how important it was, not to mention how exciting! I was getting to know myself better day by day and night by night. I was recording dreams, visions and any and all kinds of psychic experiences. Yes, it took time, effort and organization, but it was all worth it because I was learning so much and felt so much more whole.

So no matter how busy and tired you are, you must make the effort and time to meditate. You need peace and quiet to hear, see and feel the communications from the non-physical parts of your being in order to navigate a high vibrational life successfully.

## DROPPING EXPECTATIONS

When you are creating your reality consciously, expectations are not your friends. They are highly limiting because they make you vulnerable to disappointment and dissatisfaction, not to mention slow you down. When you are in the process of manifesting anything, the more open minded you are about what you wish to create, the higher the chances of getting what you want.

Let's take the example of buying your new home once again. When you imagine your dream house there are basic elements that you can specify: like the orientation of the property, the number of rooms and the method of heating and cooling for example. However, if your dream is too specific and includes the colour of the house, the exact layout of rooms, number of windows, etc, you are limiting your choices and leave no room for variations. When you leave the door open for different options, the chances of you finding a house that will suit you will be much higher.
The same goes for setting the intent to start a business, buying yourself some high priced item or planning a retirement. Once you verbalized your intent, focused on your goal, visualized, affirmed and checked your beliefs, your task is to let the Universe bring you what you asked for. Do not wonder how it is going to happen, where the money is going to come from or how you are going to do it, that is not your job. What you have to do is be awake and conscious, pay attention to your innate and your focus, and follow your gut feelings and the opportunities that arise.

What you don't do is place expectations on how this is all about to happen. With expectations you limit yourself and make it harder, if not impossible for the Universe to give you what you asked for.

I consider expectations a form of self sabotage. If you expect some things to happen a certain way you take away many routes through which the Universe could've provided you with what you desire. For example, if you believe that you can only raise money to start a business if you take a second job you will most likely find one, and through working the extra hours you will eventually come up with the funds to start your business. However, if you set the intent to have the money for it without putting expectations on how you will get it, you might not need a second job at all. You could receive the amount needed by a well funded business partner popping up, a deceased relative leaving you with an inheritance or even winning the lottery.

Another good example is when you plan to travel someplace and people who have been there before give you the lowdown on what it's like. They tell you of their experience, and depending on whether it's positive or negative it will create expectations. If you hear good things about your destination you will expect good things to happen and vice versa. However, what you have to be conscious of is that whatever you are going to experience during your travels depends on *your vibration*, not the description of others. If you heard negative things and you go in with negative expectations then that is the frequency you will be putting out, and that is the frequency the Universe is going to match.

My husband and I have heard many horror stories about New York City before we took our first trip there, and had we listened to them I don't know how our vacation would've turned out. Fortunately we chose to ignore all the negative opinions and left for the Big Apple with excitement, trusting whatever would happen. We ended up having a great trip without any problems whatsoever. We visited the US many more times, and during our travels we slept in the car in parking lots, under bridges, at rest areas and public parks, and never have been mugged, hurt or bothered in any way. We met a lot of friendly and helpful people, and that is our American experience despite all the negative stories we've heard over the years. Now that I know that it is my vibration that determines the quality of my experiences, I don't need to hear others' to create expectations.

So I suggest you drop them if you have them. Be aware, conscious, follow your instincts, common sense, and vibrate as high as you can. The Universe knows what to do. Let it do it.

## ACCEPTANCE

Spiritual teachers throughout the ages have been telling us that we must accept our circumstances before we can change them because we can't bring about a shift from a point of resistance. When you are in a situation you don't like you resist it, fight it and complain about it. All that produces a low vibration, so whatever solution you will come up with will also be of low vibration. When you find yourself in an uncomfortable place in life you first must accept your situation. You acknowledge that it's happening, accept it for the time being and that will take care of the resistance. High vibrational solutions require a high vibrational mindset, and you can't have that when you are up in arms about something. First you need to accept, cool your head, and then, from the point of a higher vibration come up with a solution.

To accept your situation for the time being is going with the flow. While you are in the flow you offer no resistance, and are able to think your way out of it. If you fight against the flow your energy will be used up for providing resistance, and that will not get you out of your predicament. I find that when I need to practice acceptance it helps if I give meaning to my situation. I look at my circumstances and make a point of finding good things about them, no matter how small. It can be as simple as *"I'm still here, kicking and I'm strong. I will work my way out of this!"*

I worked a job I didn't like for many years, and I made it meaningful because I felt that financially it was the best for me and my family. It helped to think about it as a means to put food on the table, to find challenges that brought personal satisfaction and to make friends. Once I accepted my situation and made peace with it the resistance dissolved and it was a lot easier to create happy events in my life.

## BEING PRESENT

I used to have a rich fantasy life aided by a vivid imagination. I spent a big part of my life living in my head, having some kind of an adventure, imaginary conversations or inventing some incredible stuff that saved humanity. I also spent time dwelling on past events; things that "happened to me," things I could've or should've done differently and people who hurt me. Daydreaming often gave me a lot of joy, got me through many a dreary day at my boring job, but other times it kept me resentful, teary and pained. The result of spending all this time in my head was, unfortunately, that I was on autopilot most of the time. I was still creating my reality in every second of every day, but I was doing it unconsciously, unaware, unfocused, while creating low vibrational thoughts and emotions. Instead of being present my attention was scattered all over the place, which resulted in a life of ups and downs.

This is a very common phenomenon among humanity. Not until I started awakening and learning about the importance of being in the PRESENT and consciously practising it that I noted a definite change in my life. As I worked on remaining in the present and creating my reality from the point of NOW, I experienced the quieting of my mind and the sharpening of my focus. I could direct my attention better and be consciously aware of what I was creating, how I was creating it and why.

Being present creates awareness.

We have all heard the saying: "Stop living in the past!" This is sage advice. When you live your life looking back all the time, dwelling on past events, nursing past hurts, comparing the past to the future, you are not making life choices and decisions fully present and conscious. Bringing past issues into the present will colour your emotions, beliefs, attitudes and behaviours, and thus muddy your vibration. To create the reality you want you must leave the past in the past, unless you want your present to reflect it. Dwelling on what happened before is a form of resistance, so while you are feeling guilt, remorse, resentment, pain and the like, you are not going with the flow. When you are stuck in the past your energy and consciousness spin on a low vibration until you recognize the fact that you are indeed stuck. At this point you must acknowledge it and deal with the thoughts and emotions that keep you there. Once you've cleared your issues let them go (helpful visualization techniques in the VISUALIZATION section of this book), and you will be free to bring your focus to the present and start creating your reality from this new vantage point.

Living in the present, or as it is worded in spiritual circles as "living in the NOW" has another significance: the non-linear nature of the multiverse. That means that everything, everywhere, in all levels of existence is happening at the same time. There is no past and future, everything is going on now, in the present. The world wars, the building of the pyramids of Giza and other ancient architecture, and the time of the dinosaurs walking on Earth are happening right now, just like the events of the future in probable future realities. They are all "out there," vibrating on different frequencies from our own, waiting for us to shift into when we produce a matching vibration or when we access the quantum field or Akashic Records. Time as we know it doesn't exist. It is simply a tool we use when we enter physical reality in order to structure and process our experiences while we are in an embodied state.

While living in a third dimensional environment 'timelessness' is a difficult concept for any human being. However, in most accounts of people who have experienced out of body states, projections of consciousness and other psychic phenomena, the feeling of being 'out of time' is rather prevalent. I, myself have also experienced the sensation of it while finding myself out in space during several of my earlier meditation sessions. I was out in space, "hanging there" without a body, emanating a moon-like soft, white light. All around me were thousands and thousands of stars and nothing else, and I felt like I was one of them, just being there, existing as pure light with no sense of any time passing.

I believe we are existing in this eternal present as beings of light, while at the same time we lower our vibration and express parts of ourselves into matter, into flesh and blood, and then we begin to utilize 'time' to structure our physical experiences.

## AFFIRMATIONS

There are many people who believe in the power of affirmations, and then there are those who say they don't really work. From my point of view both groups are right. Whether affirmations work for you or not depends on how you are doing it.

All the effort you put into verbalizing your affirmations will be worth nothing if there is no belief and conviction behind them. It is one thing to say the words and quite another to actually mean and believe them. This is a tricky one because it requires you to believe in the existence of something that hasn't materialized in your reality *yet*. This is where the significance of being awake, aware and conscious comes in.

It's important to remember that we are multi-dimensional beings, living multidimensional lives in a multidimensional Universe or Multiverse. We exist in an infinite number of alternate/parallel realities all at once, constantly shifting between them as we make a multitude of decisions in every single moment of every day. What that means is that there are variations of our reality existing "out there," waiting for us to make the choice to shift there. For example, if you are dreaming of one day running your own business, know that there are so called unmanifested probable realities in existence where you've already achieved that. Now it's "only" a matter of setting your intention, focusing, following your nudges, and when you are vibrating *I'm running a business!* shifting there. When you know that your dream already exists and is waiting for you to "get it" it is not that difficult to believe in your affirmations. You have to dismiss any doubts, and affirm what you already know, that what you are working towards ALREADY EXISTS!

An excellent example of this is this very book I'm writing. Once I had the idea for it I set the intention to get it started. This is what it sounded like when I verbalized it:

*"It is my intent to write a book, one that will help others successfully create the kind of reality for themselves they dream about."*

Then, as I began writing my notes I started saying my affirmations, and I intend to keep that up throughout the entire writing process. This is the affirmation I'm using:

*"I have a book published! It is based on my personal experiences, and is helping a great number of people who want to awaken to the nature of reality and to their own power. My book is available for sale and it teaches others how they can create their reality when they are awakened, aware and conscious."*

In order to bring my dream into reality I use all the tools available to me. I visualize my book already written, for sale in the stores, in people's shopping carts and sitting on my bookshelf. I put no expectations on how it should go, how long the book should be or the colour of the cover, whether it will be published by a publisher or by myself. I know these things will all work out in their own time. Remember, expectations are limiting so the less I have the better. It also helps that I have never written a book before and have no idea what publishing it will involve. As they say, I will cross that bridge when I come to it. All I care about is that I'm doing it, I feel great about it, and I know that in a probable reality my book has already been published, people are reading it as we speak and find it very helpful. If you are reading this book that means that through this conscious creating process I have accomplished what I set out to do, and learning from my example you can do the same.

I'm a firm believer in the benefits of positive affirmations, general ones as well as those we do during our process of manifestation. By verbalizing them we acknowledge and strengthen our trust in our power as eternal beings of light and reality creators, and overwrite old, often limiting beliefs that sabotage our efforts.

Positive affirmations are very popular today. They can be found in many places: books, websites and apps. Here are a few I've used in the past, some I find very helpful:

*"I can do anything when I set my mind to it."*
*"I'm a healthy person, I'm immune to ill health."*
*"Every day I'm getting better and better."*
*"Things always work out for me."*
*"Nothing is impossible."*
*"I always have enough money."*
*"I always meet friendly and helpful people wherever I go."*
*"Whatever happens in life, I'm always going to be okay."*

I have been using these affirmations for many years, and by today they've become reflections of my reality. My advice is that you pick or create for yourself a few of them that will serve to keep you in a positive mindset, feeling empowered at all times, and stick with them. I don't know if reading different affirmations every day from many different sources really works, but I can vouch for the ones I chose all those years ago. They are the handful that accompanied me on my journey from the very beginning until today.

Again, the disclaimer I have to make here is that there is always the matter of your soul contract, a so called karma, and the purpose of you deciding to take a brave leap into this incredibly dense 3D playground. If you, for example were born into physical reality to experience the dynamics of poverty and lack, then you might come in with certain restrictions. Once you've gained enough experience though or you have learned what you came here to learn you can cancel your contract, drop your karma, and then as they say, anything goes!

How do you cancel your contract or drop your karma? You do this the same way you do everything else: by verbalizing your intent, knowing that your subconscious (your Higher Self) and the Universe, God, Source or All That Is, whichever name you prefer, is always listening (in other words, receiving your vibration and reading your frequency) and is always there to do your bidding. And then you work hard on raising your vibration. Once your frequency is high enough these third dimensional things will fall away anyway. So your best bet is to be always on the highest vibration you can be.

*Chapter 5*

# MORE TOOLS AND PRACTICES OF CONSCIOUS REALITY CREATION

There are a great number of other useful practices you can apply to raise your vibration and keep it high. The more of them you use the better results you will see.

### POSITIVE ATTITUDE

As they say, the right attitude is half the battle won. When you look at life and choose to focus on the beauty and greatness of it more and the hardships and struggle less, you vibrate on a higher frequency and you will attract higher vibrational events and people into your reality. That doesn't mean that you remain blissfully ignorant of the world's ills and turn your back on them, rather, quite the opposite. Once you acknowledged their existence you can take steps to improve those conditions by creating the highest vibrational version of yourself you can. As you radiate your frequency wherever you go you are affecting people everywhere in your path, helping them raise their vibration as well. You can also help out physically: donate money, work with the homeless and feed the hungry. These are all a tremendous help for those who struggle with everyday existence, but the best you can do for yourself and others is that you diligently work on raising your own vibration.

Some people are born with a positive attitude, for others it's something they have to learn and work at. They have to train themselves to see the bright side of things instead of the dark, to pay attention to the positive events in their environment and the world, not to the disasters, terrorist acts, scandals and the like that the world news is usually full of. What you pay attention to strongly affects your reality, so do yourself a favour and keep your eyes and mind on the positive stuff.

Here are a few examples of having a positive attitude:

*"Things always work out for me."*
*"I have the power to accomplish anything."*
*"Everywhere I go I find friendly, helpful people."*
*"I'm not feeling the greatest right now but I know it's only temporary. I will feel better soon."*
*"No matter their past, people can change for the better any time."*
*"I'm not good at this yet, but with learning and practice I will improve."*
*"It's okay to make mistakes, they help us learn."*

Negative attitude:

*"The world is rotten, it will never get better."*
*"Life sucks."*
*"There is never a free parking space."*
*"I bet there will be a lineup when we get there."*
*"No matter what you do, you always get screwed."*
*"Everybody is after your money."*

A negative attitude is a low vibrational attribute that will bring people and events into your life that match that frequency. So you want to watch your thoughts, opinions and general attitude towards everything and everybody. There is a difference between seeing and acknowledging the problems in the world and writing it all off as a bad job that cannot be improved.

I'd like to mention here another detail to watch for: not every negative thought comes from you. As we live our lives and interact with others we are constantly exposing them to our energy, influencing them with our vibrations, and it is also true the other way around. The ethers are full of the thoughts of humanity, a lot of it negative, and we pick them up with our rather sensitive internal antennae. We are also affected by energies from other non-physical realities, so we pick up thoughts and ideas from this invisible soup that affect our thoughts and moods if we don't pay attention to it. That is why it's so important to observe the thoughts that enter our minds, to recognize the ones that seem out of place and weed them out.

When you operate on a higher vibration in your everyday life, the low frequency thoughts and energies of others have a harder time to reach and affect you, therefore it is easier to keep yourself in a positive mindset that influences your general attitude.

## ELIMINATING LIMITING BELIEFS

Limiting beliefs are those that cause us to restrict ourselves in some way. Some of them were attached to us during childhood and might be hiding in our subconscious. Others we developed as adults, and they are generally stemming from low self esteem or fear of getting out of our comfort zone.
Some of the most common limiting beliefs are:

*"I'm not good or smart enough."*
*"I'm too young/old for this."*
*"You need money to make money."*
*"I'll never be successful."*
*"I don't have what it takes to become what I want to be."*

Having these limiting beliefs either in your subconscious or out in the open will undermine your ability to create your desired event because they are a part of your overall frequency. Before you begin the process of conscious manifesting you have to make sure that you are aware of the contents of your mind, including the many beliefs you hold, and get rid of the ones that don't serve you.

## NO JUDGEMENT

Judging ourselves and others is a rather prevalent human trait, one that doesn't do any good to anybody. When you judge yourself negatively you are actively chopping away at your self esteem, resulting in thinking less of yourself. When judging others you place yourself above them, measure their actions and behaviours by your own ideas, morals and belief systems, suggesting that theirs are inferior to yours.

Judgements are more often than not a result of past or present social and cultural conditioning, things learned in childhood, or they come from an unhealthy ego. Just like gossip they do little for anyone, except keep people in low vibration.

If tempted to make a negative judgement about anyone or anything, remember that you don't know what drives them. Most often you don't know their culture, their personal circumstances, their struggles, their past or present. You don't know what kind of contract they were born with and the type of challenges they set up for themselves to experience in physical reality. Also, in the media most times we only get shown one side of a story. The other remains a mystery so we cannot see the full picture, without which it is impossible to create a balanced opinion.

My approach to all this is to live and let live. I have the right and the opportunity to create my reality freely, as does everybody else on this planet.

## OVERCOMING PAST CONDITIONING AND OUTDATED BELIEFS

Every single one of us have been conditioned since childhood to think and act certain ways: according to our parents' beliefs and morals, our culture's customs and society's expectations. This conditioning served a purpose for a while, but when you become conscious you realize that a lot of things that you were taught in your youth or even later not just no longer make sense, but are also pretty harmful, limiting, or plain ignorant.

My father used to teach me that in life it is best if we live like a grey little mouse. According to him that way we will not be noticed, singled out or bothered by anyone in any way. I lived by that preconditioned belief until my thirties, when I began awakening and realized that those were the words of a man who lived his whole life in communism. That attitude may have served him, but it was not applicable to a young woman such as myself at the time, and it was certainly not conductive to the development of a healthy self esteem. He also told me repeatedly that a man (or woman) must make something out of himself by the time he is 40, because after that he will never get anything going. This was a rather common belief where I come from back in those days. Well, here I am, 58 years old, writing my first book, thinking: *"Dad, I think you were wrong about that one!"*

Here are a few more beliefs that were rather prevalent in my time:

*"You have to work hard if you want to live well!"*

*"It's a man's job to woo a woman not the other way around,"* or *"women shouldn't initiate a relationship, it's not decent."*

*"You will never get ahead in life if you are not street smart."*

*"It is selfish to think of yourself before others."*

And how about this one: *"It is wrong to get up from the table until you finished all your food!"* A great many of us grew up with that one. I figure it was a leftover (no pun intended) attitude from a time when food was scarce. Today, that old conditioning can be a cause for several eating disorders.

We have all grown up with these kind of outdated and limiting ideas and beliefs, and they had a tremendous influence on our thinking and behaviour. When we take a closer look at our own attitudes we often find that a lot of them are carryovers from our parents' and grandparents' era and are no longer relevant in modern times. Therefore it is important to actually hear what we say and weed our ancestors' outdated beliefs out of our own.

## VERBALIZATION

Words have tremendous power. Our ancestors knew it, ancient civilizations knew it, and it is time that we remembered it.

I'm a firm believer in the power and effectiveness of verbalization. Whether it's intent, affirmation or gratitude, I like to say them out loud. Since I live with several other people in my household, most of whom are skeptical about pretty much anything spiritual, I choose not to do my verbalizations at home. Several times a week I head out for a walk and find places where talking to myself will not attract anyone's attention. I say my intent and affirmations out loud which reinforces the sensation that I'm being heard, and that strengthens my conviction that whatever I'm asking for will be provided for me. Verbalizing my gratitude is also important to me, because I want the Universe to know that I appreciate all the help given to me every day of my life.

## SELF OBSERVATION

I learned a long time ago that it is not what you see in the news and in the world that matters, it's how you react to it and what you think about it.

When you start observing your reactions you will find that they are good indicators of the level of your vibration. Are you paying more attention to positive or negative events? How do you react to disasters, violence and reports of corruption? Do you experience anger, frustration, fear, a desire to punish people or feel exasperated because you see humanity as the scourge of the planet?

As I slowly awakened throughout the years I observed my reactions to events, situations I found myself in, the behaviours of others and things I watched and read, and noticed a significant change as I was slowly rising in vibration. Before, I reacted with anger, frustration and dismay at a lot of things I encountered or read about. As I was gradually awakening I began to realize that there is a bigger picture here that I have to look at closely and consciously.

Learning from a vast amount of spiritual and metaphysical material and my own experiences, I had to acknowledge the existence of soul contracts that work both individually and on the world stage. Famous people and world leaders all come in with their own purpose, contracts and challenges, just like everyone else. They can play the part of a good, charismatic and caring leader or a dictator and everything else in between, depending on the life lesson they came here to learn or help teach, for they are also a part of other people's contract. For example, if you came in to this third dimensional reality to experience life in a dictatorship, you needed a "co-star" in your play who would act out the part of the evil leader. Before you were born you found a willing fellow light being who volunteered to take the part for their own learning experience, thus the contract was made.

Every light being who was born into this Earth experience came in voluntarily with contracts, and is willingly (although obliviously because of the amnesia) playing out their life purpose. The participants of all disasters, wars, dictatorships, accidents, etc. all knew what they were volunteering for. We have to be aware of that when we look at the world around us and react to what we see.

With awareness comes understanding. The more you understand the nature of reality and the participants' role in it, the more your reaction to world events and personal experiences will change. When you practice self observation you see not just the world around you but also yourself in it, how you relate to it and how it relates to you. Once you recognize and acknowledge the existence of soul contracts, you will look at everything through a lens of understanding and grace. The feeling of anger, dismay, devastation and the desire to see people punished gives way to compassion, understanding and gratitude, all of which are high vibrational attitudes.

To practice self observation you can start with pausing in your activities for a few minutes whenever you have the time and take stock of your present. Ask yourself: *"What am I doing right now? What am I thinking and saying? What am I paying attention to? What are my present circumstances? Is there anything lowering my vibration right now? Do I have any issues I need to deal with?"* Observe yourself as you go about your day to day life, the attitudes and emotions you feel and consider their source. Think about the people around you at home, in your extended family, among friends, at work, and consider your connection to them. If there are issues between you is it because they are mirroring your vibration, or do you feel there is a "contract action" going on between you. Observe yourself in relation to others and yourself.

What is your relationship with yourself? Do you accept and love yourself? Are you comfortable with who you are? Do you appreciate the efforts you make every day to deal with your life, or do you feel a lack of self esteem and wish you were doing better? Do you acknowledge and feel good about your accomplishments, or do you pay more attention to your perceived failures?

The world is full of people who look down on themselves and make comparisons to others all the time, feel weak and undeserving because they often struggle to cope with their life. They feel envious because others seem to be doing so much better than them. They would think so much more of themselves if they were conscious of who they are, where they come from and what kind of life purpose and challenges they came in with. It takes a great deal of courage and strength to come into this reality for a life full of hardships and trauma, cope with it, let alone turn it around for the better. People with simple, relatively easy lives often judge and criticize others who struggle with abuse, addictions and many other kinds of life challenges, not realizing that it takes a lot more effort, fortitude and determination to deal with a life full of challenges, than with one that is relatively smooth sailing.

## COMMUNICATING WITH THE NON-PHYSICAL

Communicating with the non-physical parts of our existence is going on all the time, continuously, whether we are consciously aware of it or not. There is never a time when we are left alone, abandoned, untethered or separated in any way from our greater self and the Universe. Due to our amnesia in this dense reality many people feel alone and unloved, unaware of their greater self and the vast network of consciousnesses ready to assist behind the curtains.

There are people who are consciously aware of their connection to the non-physical Universe. Some have been since they were born, others developed their inner sense for it later in life. Then there are those who have remained unaware that they have a greater existence outside of the third dimensional reality they've known all their life and are completely oblivious to their multidimensional nature. Nevertheless, aware or not, we are in communication with our greater self all the time. We receive energy, communication, healing, information downloads and the "nudges" that steer us throughout our journey. When we are conscious and aware we communicate back through meditation and verbalization.

It is important to pay attention to and recognize the communications from the non-physical, for they are sent to assist us in either keeping ourselves on our path, or sometimes just to jolt us out of certain emotional states that are not in our best interest. I have discovered a pattern of this during my awakening, when I would get worked up over something while peeling potatoes for dinner for example. I would quietly fume and argue with someone in my head, then the knife would slip and cut my finger, and that would effectively interrupt the stream of angry thoughts. I've been jolted out of internal tantrums this way many times in my life, and once I became conscious I recognized these events for what they were. Instead of getting even more angry about cutting my finger, tripping on a rock or slipping on the ice, these days I just stop right there and ask myself: *"What was I just thinking about? What was this warning for? What kind of thought or behaviour am I trying to bring attention to?"*

I learned some time ago that these kind of small accidents - or even bigger ones - are communications from the Universe, and their purpose is to help us stay on course or bring our attention to something important.

Again, I'd like to mention the importance of quieting the mind, for when your head is constantly full of thoughts, commentaries and opinions, you have a hard time hearing and feeling the messages that are coming through. Meditation quiets the noise and allows the non-physical information to come in.

## CHOOSING THE COMPANY WE KEEP

In our quest to raise our vibration and keep a high frequency, one of the best things we can do for ourselves is to carefully choose the company we keep. Just like we are affecting others with our level of vibration they are influencing us the same way, so we need to be watchful of the levels of vibration we allow ourselves to interact with. Therefore it is a good idea to surround yourself with cheerful, positive, helpful and friendly people who have your best interest at heart. Toxic friendships and relationships will drag you down emotionally, and they will keep you in a low vibration. It is best to either let them go or limit your exposure to them.

When you come up with an idea and talk about it with others you will find yourself facing two kinds of people:

ones whose face will light up and start making suggestions on how to make it happen and offer to help, and others who will screw up their faces, shake their heads and tell you a list of reasons why they think it's not a good idea and why it will not work. I suggest that you stay close to the first group while politely ignoring the second.

As you go about your life you meet all kinds of people: those who look at life with a positive attitude and whose glass is always half full, those that enthusiastically seek solutions to problems, and those who complain all the time and lament on how hard and unfair life is. You will recognize the ones that are high vibrational by their aura of peace and wisdom, and sometimes you feel their energy bubbling around you. You feel good being around them. Those are the people whose company you seek. At the same time, acknowledge and respect those whom are not yet awake and conscious, for their path may not be the same as yours and their journey harder.

## THE TAMING OF THE EGO

If I had to pick one attribute of the human being that is the most capable of keeping a person in a low vibration, it would be the ego. Our ego was designed for the purpose of assisting us in the navigation of our environment and to keep us safe. Not just our physical bodies but our emotions as well. Its task is to keep us from getting hurt in any way.

However, in unhealthy doses the ego tends to run amok and the result of that is a human displaying characteristics such as anger, arrogance, defensiveness, contempt, judgement, criticism, jealousy, abuse, violence, a lust for power and control.

The ego unchecked can and will keep you in a low vibration so it has to be tamed. You must pay close attention to your opinions and reactions. Once you are conscious and aware you will feel it when they are ego based because you will observe yourself getting triggered. As you "hit back" at someone whose words or actions activated your negative reaction you will recognize your ego's self defence mechanism at work.

There is a vast amount of literature written about how to keep one's ego in check. I find that the most effective way is to keep raising your vibration and the ego's hold will start to slacken. You will know it's working when you notice that you are losing interest in responding to low vibrational remarks or behaviours from others. You will no longer wish to engage in negative banter, office gossip, comparisons and arguments. You will set boundaries and walk away from ego based interactions. As you are raising your vibration and move away from your ego making the decisions for you, you might notice that people around you will either begin to change or start to drop away from you. Those that no longer match your frequency will have no place in your life, and they will be replaced by others who are on your level of vibration.

## LIVE AND LET LIVE

As you begin your journey of awakening you might find a number of obstacles in your path, some of which are going to be people whose attitude towards you is: "*I just don't get it.*" They probably have known you for some time, and as you are changing they see you turning into a new person, someone who is no longer on the same wavelength as they are, someone strange and different. What's worse, you are talking about things they either don't understand or don't agree with, so they no longer know what to make of you. I have met a number of those on my journey and thankfully most of them were willing to humour me. They let me go on about my psychic adventures, my new ways of looking at my own existence and life in general, then shrugged and went about their business. Others suggested I was dreaming or imagining my psychic experiences.

If you are walking this path, chances are that you have your own stories to tell about the skeptic attitude of others watching your transformation. Maybe they called you weird, said you've gone 'round the bend or thought you are losing your mind. Whatever is the case, it does not matter. Your focus must be on your own life, your work, the progress you are making and your goals. As I mentioned before, every single person has incarnated on this planet and at this time for their own reasons. They have their own purpose, contracts and challenges. It doesn't matter if they don't understand yours or you theirs, everyone walks their own path.

Imagine that you are excitedly telling someone about a spiritual experience you had. They give you 'The Look' and say they don't believe you. What are you going to do? If you are a high vibrational person you will smile, wish them well and move on. You understand that others are on a different path, and from their point of view your story can very well be nonsensical. If you are on a low vibration your ego will jump into action, your hackles will rise with resentment about how they reacted to your wondrous story and an argument will ensue. Before you know it all your excitement is gone, your vibration is under the bottom of your feet and your mood is ruined for the rest of the day.

What is the lesson here? Take the high road. The opinion and attitude of others don't matter, only yours. Remember the golden rule: **The disbelief of others does not negate your experience.** You know what you saw or experienced and that is all the validation you need. Don't look for it from any other sources.


## KNOWING YOUR POWER

We have been taught all our lives how small and insignificant we are in the vastness of the universe. We were told that we are nothing but a grain of sand in the desert, a single drop in the ocean. It took me over four decades to realize how absolutely not true that is. Once we awaken to our true nature we realize how much bigger and more significant we are than we've ever known, and recognize the tremendous amount of power we hold within us. With the help of those who have awakened before us and dedicated their life to teach us what they knew, we can learn about our true nature and how to use this power to create a desirable reality for ourselves. Once we understand and experience how our thoughts, beliefs and attitudes affect the things that "happen to us" and how the Universe answers to our frequency, we are no longer operating in the dark. We are no longer the victims of circumstances, and never again are we waiting for a higher power to rescue us from our predicament because we know that it is Us.

It took me a long time to recognize and understand my own power. During the years I was learning and experimenting I went through a number of stages until I recognized and accepted myself as the creator of my reality.

At first I thought I was just lucky. I had to be, because my dreams - no matter how "crazy" or "impossible" - tended to come true. Also, I seemed to always get out of trouble and end up being okay no matter what situation I got myself into. So whenever I dreamed up something and it materialized I declared myself the luckiest girl on the planet. Then I began learning about conscious reality creation and started experimenting, and as things kept coming together to my advantage it dawned on me that there was only so long I could keep calling all this luck and coincidence. At one point I had to come to terms with the fact that I was the one actually "doing it," there really was no miracle going on there. I was consciously, deliberately and knowingly creating my reality.

Once you come into your power use it every chance you get, for practice makes the master. Use it to keep yourself in the highest vibration you can be, to bring your dreams into reality, and to help awaken those whom are ready and willing to do so. Remember, you are broadcasting your frequency everywhere you go, affecting everything and everyone. Now that is power. Use it well.

## NON-INTERFERENCE

Up until now I talked about how to consciously create our own reality, but what about that of others? Isn't it selfish to pay all this attention to and do all this work on our own life and ignore the reality of others? To what degree can we involve ourselves into the lives of our fellow humans? When we contemplate these questions there are several things we have to keep in mind:

1. First of all, there is the matter of soul contract. Before we are born into a physical vehicle we decide the parameters of our Earth experience, a life purpose and the challenges we are planning to face. We plan these things

individually and in groups. Once we are born we begin to play out these challenges and continue on throughout our lives until we gained experience and raised our vibration high enough to "get it." So when we see people struggling with issues, along with the desire to help we must also have the understanding that they are living out their challenges, just like we are experiencing our own. That doesn't mean we don't help wherever we can, but knowing that others are dealing with personal life issues and events they designed for themselves for their own learning goes a long way in understanding the validity of their experiences.

2. Another well known saying is that "before we can help others, we must learn to help ourselves." In the context of this book, this means that we have to learn and work on raising our vibration and become conscious creators of our reality before we can involve ourselves in others' process with advice. Before we awaken and become aware we tend to look for third dimensional solutions to our problems, and that leaves us in the 3D paradigm which we are working to rise out of by raising our vibration.

Let's take an example of a situation with a woman who keeps getting into abusive relationships. What advice would we give her? The 3D advice is for her to try to make better judgements when it comes to potential romantic partners. The high vibrational advice is to encourage her to become conscious, look inside of herself and recognize both the low vibrational aspects of her that are drawing negative experiences into her life, as well as the soul contract based nature of the play she is acting out. Once she has identified those traits she can work on them, and as she brings herself up to a higher vibration she will draw more appropriate partners to herself.

Until we learn to think of higher vibrational solutions we will give lower vibrational advice to others.

3. When you become conscious and realize the significance of what you know, as a lightworker your first instinct is to try and teach others so they could have an easier life just like you do. However, you will soon see that not everyone is ready for this information.

The people of Earth are awakening at their own time and pace. Some will be interested in what you have to say but others have not gotten to that point yet. In my youth I was definitely not ready. I would've laughed all of this stuff off as a joke. As a matter of fact I did, because I was absolutely science minded and considered all spiritual, supernatural and paranormal phenomena religious nonsense at worst, and *"I've never seen it so I don't know what to make of it"* at best. Only in my mid thirties, after getting triggered to awaken during my Arizona trip I expressed the first sign of interest in anything spiritual. So no matter how enthusiastic you are and how much you would like to guide and help others, some people will simply not be ready to listen to what you have to say because they have not gotten to the point in their life where they would be receptive to your information. There are also those who will not choose to awaken in this incarnation at all because they still have a lot of learning and experiencing to do.

By talking about your awakening you are planting seeds that will sprout as time goes by, and more and more people will need assistance as they become ready for more information. If you see that there is no interest in your advice or you find resistance to your words, let it go and walk away. Set an example and wait for others to come to you when they are ready, and come they will, when they see how you've sorted yourself out and are living the kind of life you wanted for yourself.

## MINDING YOUR ENERGY

We are all made of conscious energy, vibrating on different levels of consciousness. Throughout our lifetime we put our energy into everything we do and therefore affect everything and everyone in our environment.

The energy of your words influence your audience, just like your moods affect the company around you. The vibration of what you are thinking and feeling while cooking goes into your food and affects those who eat it. Your energy is absorbed by the objects you touch or make and it affects those who come into contact with them.

Since it works the other way around as well, it is a good idea to be mindful of what kind of energies you allow to influence you. That means recognizing low vibrational people, actions and events in your environment and keeping your distance from them. Keeping your vibration high at all times helps keep your energy "clean."

## ACCEPTING AND APPRECIATING YOURSELF

One of the most intriguing observations I've made throughout my lifetime about myself and my fellow human beings is how many of us don't value, accept and appreciate ourselves; how many don't recognize the effort, the strength and perseverance it requires to exist in our difficult reality, and the sheer willpower needed to meet our challenges, overcome them and turn our life around. How much effort it requires sometimes just to stay in the same place and keep one's sanity. Thanks to those outdated attitudes, beliefs, morals and generally low vibrational thinking I talked about earlier, it is our presumed "failures" and "weaknesses" society tends to focus and dwell on, instead of the tremendous amount of effort people everywhere put into the building and maintaining of their lives.

Fortunately these kind of old school attitudes are slowly going out the window, and people are generally getting better at not just recognizing and appreciating their own efforts in coping with their life challenges, but that of their fellow humans' as well. The criticizing of others to make one's self feel superior is slowly giving way to expressing understanding and support.

When creating our reality consciously, one of the greatest things we can do for ourselves is to recognize the tremendous amount of courage, fortitude, patience and determination it takes to live lifetimes "after" lifetimes in a third dimensional physical reality. Regardless of how many times we feel that we are weak, lost our way or failed in any way, the fact that we are here and doing it is a testament to our strength, willpower and tenacity. So whenever you find yourself struggling or feeling down, powerless and ready to declare defeat, remember what an incredibly courageous and strong person you are, and what a great group of helpers and supporters stand behind you, waiting for you to ask for help. Know that those times of desperation are mere stepping stones towards something so much greater!

Many people, myself included, regularly express our gratitude towards the Universe, God, Source or Spirit for our existence, our accomplishments, and the help we receive throughout our everyday life. Next time you are giving thanks don't forget to express your appreciation for yourself as well, for you are doing a great service to the Universe by being here, living your life, interacting with others, and just being *You*. *Y*ou are learning and teaching others through your words, actions and your vibrations, as you shine your light wherever you go.

## USING HIGH VIBRATIONAL SOLUTIONS TO EVERYDAY ISSUES

Whenever we run into any kind of problem there is always a choice about how to react to it. We can produce either a low or a high vibrational reaction. A low vibrational reaction is when we get angry and frustrated, complain to whoever is willing to listen and blame somebody. A high vibrational reaction is to acknowledge the issue and start looking for solutions.

As you raise your vibration the bigger dramas fall away, but you will still encounter smaller nuisances that will test you. Whenever I run into one of those I notice that I still try to think of a 3D solution first, then I shake my head and move on to a high vibe method to deal with it. Old habits die hard and I still have to work at remembering that I now have a better way of handling the small issues.

Let's take an example of a noisy neighbour. I certainly have experience with those. For whatever reason I have created them a number of times in my life. The way I used to deal with this problem was that I huffed and puffed, complained to everyone around me, until I could take it no more and had a polite, friendly talk with the neighbours. That quieted them for a couple of days then they started up again. It would go on like this for months, even years. Now I do it this way: I talk to them first and if they quiet down, that's good. If not, I set my intent to live in peace and quiet and visualize myself enjoying the silence in my neighbourhood. I verbalize my intent and affirmation:

*"I intend/love living here with friendly neighbours, in a quiet and peaceful environment!"*

I work on this for a couple of days, weeks or longer and then wait to see what happens. I might even verbalize a request to the Universe to help me with my problem. The result of doing it the high vibrational way is that either the neighbours do something about their noise, or at one point I find that they don't really bother me that much anymore, or both.

Again, it's important to not have expectations with what you are creating. You have to be open to whatever kind of solution that comes that will solve or at least ease your problem. Of course, the ideal situation is if the neighbours go silent. It could happen but remember, they are people whom are not yet awakened therefore not aware, or are uncaring of the well being of those around them and they want to enjoy their life just like everyone else. For many people that includes loud parties, booming music, revving motorcycle engines, or like in my case, running a noisy hot tub motor.

So if you find yourself in a similar situation you can try two ways: deal with the problem physically or mentally. If you do it in the physical 3D way you might find an unresponsive or hostile neighbour and you could get into arguments and lawsuits, all of which are going to keep you angry and frustrated and in low vibration. My suggestion is that you deal with it using high vibe methods. I find that they work for me.

All of this requires clear intent, work and discipline. It is very easy to fall back into the old ways but you will find them unsatisfactory. Once you do the work and see the result, this way of handling things becomes the routine not the exception. I use this method for all issues that arise in my life with excellent results.

Another thought to consider here is that noisy neighbours, a bad boss and other circumstances that can aggravate and frustrate you might not be a result of low vibration or the Universe testing you. They might very well be a nudge from your innate that it is time to move on, make a change, move to a different neighbourhood or get a new job, because that is what serves your highest good.

Yes I know, it all sounds pretty complicated, but remember, the more you raise your vibration the more conscious and aware you become. The more attention you pay to yourself and your circumstances as you observe yourself navigating life, the more you realize the correlation between your thoughts, beliefs and your creations. You will understand the 'why's and the 'how's, and you will know when you are getting the nudge that will show you which way to go.

*Chapter 6*

# THE BENEFITS OF CONSCIOUS, HIGH VIBRATIONAL LIVING

Living your everyday life consciously as much of the time as possible takes a lot of work at the beginning of your transformation. However, with practice and self discipline you will master this skill, and keeping yourself in high vibration and conscious throughout your days will eventually become a habit that requires very little effort. Here are some of the advantages of conscious, high vibrational living:

<u>No more drama</u>
When you are continuously vibrating on a high frequency, the unpredictable ups-and-downs nature of your life turns into a steady flow. There is a lot less turbulence, and those who try to continue to cause drama either change with you or disappear from your life completely.

Inner peace
As the drama disappears from your life you feel an inner peace envelop you that will surprise you. You find that things no longer bother or worry you the way they used to. You are able to look at issues with an emotional detachment if you choose to, and you observe and measure but never judge.

Good health
You enjoy a general sense of well being, have lots of energy, and common diseases rarely find you. They are a third dimensional construct, and once you move into the higher frequencies they won't be able to connect to you.

Successful creation of desired elements of everyday life
Goals are achieved, dreams come true. Things going in the direction you want them to and working out to your advantage.

Living with a sense of security
As you become aware of your multidimensional nature and your everlasting connection to the Universe, you know deep inside that you are and always will be safe and taken care of, and you are never, ever alone.

Seeing the world around you change with you
The higher your frequency the more high vibrational people and events come into your life. Toxic friendships

and relationships fall away and are replaced by people who will support you and enrich your life.

<u>Empowerment</u>
You are in the driver's seat of your life and you know it! It fills you with a sense of strength and confidence. You find that there are very few things you cannot do or are afraid of.

After talking about the advantages of living life on a high vibration we have to also consider the disadvantages of the opposite. The consequences of low vibrational living encompass all aspects of one's reality: moods, health, finances, security, etc.

These are some of the pitfalls of a low vibrational existence:

<u>Drama</u>
Everyday life full of drama and turbulence that take the forms of domestic issues, workplace conflicts and accidents. A continuous succession of ups and downs. Something is always going on.

<u>Lethargy</u>
Lack of energy and a general sense of non-wellbeing. Feeling tired of work, hardships and life in general.

## Victimhood
Desired goals not coming together and things not working out, resulting in the feeling of being the victim of "bad luck" and circumstances.

## Ailments
Negative emotions, stress and underlying inner issues causing different kinds of illnesses.

## Fear
The constant presence of fear and uncertainty. Worrying about the present, the future, finances, health, etc.

## Addictions
Being stuck in an endless loop of drug, alcohol and other types of abuse.

*Chapter 7*

**MASS CONSCIOUSNESS**

Just like there is individual consciousness, there is also group and mass consciousness. As we established before, the higher the number of consciousnesses who focus on a single issue, the more power they give it. The mass consciousness of humanity has tremendous power in creating and influencing events and circumstances, be it natural, political or economical. A large number of people working on a common purpose can create changes, influence natural events, or keep unwanted circumstances going by focusing on them. Mass activities have the power to raise or lower the frequency of the mass consciousness of humanity.

Here are some of the most common **unconscious, low vibrational** mass activities:

## Gossiping

Whether it's at home, at the office, at the store or online, people gossip everywhere. It is an ego based activity that can be harmful to both the gossipers and the gossipee. It can involve judgement, malevolence, envy, jealousy, all low vibe attributes, and if repeatedly aimed at the same person it could very well qualify as abuse. It can harm the target's self esteem, dignity, and mental and emotional well being. Gossipers end up hurting not just another person but themselves as well, for by gossiping they keep themselves in a low vibration.

## Online arguments

With the world wide web opening the communication arena for people all over the world, online mass arguments have developed and exploded in our present times. With so many participants from so many backgrounds of ethnicity, education, morals and beliefs bringing many points of views and opinions to the table (all of them believing that their truth is the one that counts), it is no surprise that cyberspace is full of bitter disputes and angry voices pretty much all of the time. I call this era the rise of the human ego, because it is the culprit of all the arrogance and grandstanding that is so prevalent in online communities and forums today.

## The casting of judgements

This one is similar to gossip but it deserves its own space because it's so rampant everywhere. Before the internet there were the so called gossip and celebrity rags. Now we have Facebook and numerous other websites that make their living with creating content that invites the masses to express their opinions about people's lives, actions, and even words. For the many with an overactive ego this is a great opportunity to display their perceived superiority of values and morals, with utter disregard of those of the subjects'.


## The consumption of low vibrational entertainment

Millions of people all over the world regularly watch news and movies every day. The movies can be a source of a lot of joy, fun and laughter, or a great deal of low vibrational energy. Unfortunately in the last decade or two the popularity of violent, bloody shows exploded, creeping into children's entertainment as well, spreading low vibrational content everywhere. The major focus of the news is mostly negative events all over the world, wars, disasters, accidents and disputes, adding to the already low vibrational quality of other sources of entertainment.

## Complaining

This one is probably more widespread than all the others put together. People love to complain about themselves, others, life and the state of the world in general. It is easy to observe that when people call each other up to ask "How are you?" the conversation usually turns into complaints of issues and misfortunes pretty fast. As they say, misery loves company, but it has drawbacks; the complainers may feel temporarily better after unloading their burden on an unsuspecting recipient, but this way they pass on their low vibrational emotions to another who otherwise may have been in good spirits before the phone call. If they both like to complain then they keep a steady flow of negativity between them, thus feeding the low vibe off of each other. I have noticed this trait in myself as well and had to work at learning to cut the whining off as soon as I heard it leave my lips, or even better, before the words had a chance to form.

Some of the most common **conscious, high vibrational** mass activities:

## Mass meditations

I have participated in a number of these and their effect is phenomenal. When one person focuses on a goal it is a powerful and effective way of creating one's reality. When more consciousnesses band together and focus on a common goal the power of their effects multiply. Imagine the positive effect of millions of people meditating on peace, health, the well being of humanity, our planet Earth and all of her creatures, great and small! This is how we bring much needed change to our world, individually and en masse by raising our vibration. As the frequency of our mass reality rises, the wars, the poverty, the suffering and all the low vibrational attributes of our existence in physical reality fall away.

Many people wonder if it counts as participating in a mass meditation if they watch the meditation program later. Since time is not linear it does not matter whether we meditate with the thousands who tuned in to the program when it aired or do it at a later time. We are still part of that meditation and our consciousness adds to its effectiveness.

## Creating and participating in online and in-person teaching and congregating platforms with positive, empowering messages

Before the internet (if anybody old enough still remembers) we had great spiritual teachers writing us books, some appearing in interviews on TV shows and running workshops in different cities all over the world. It was a great (though for many not very affordable) way to spread knowledge and bring people of similar vibration and spiritual beliefs together. Today, thanks to the world wide web there are a large number of platforms established to freely teach and guide the many people eager to receive information and to learn. Thanks to this, the awakening masses no longer have to search for answers while wandering in the dark by themselves like many in my generation did. There is information available everywhere for those who look. Some say there is too much of it now and a lot of it is misleading, but this is where everyone must use discernment and only accept information that matches their vibration and feels appropriate.

## The application of non-traditional energy and quantum based healing modalities

One of the fastest growing attribute of the spiritual revolution happening today is the development and application of new (and some not so new) energy and quantum healing modalities. More and more awakening people are becoming conscious of their multidimensional nature, the connection between their mental and emotional states and the well-being of their bodies, as well as the importance of vibration and frequency in both healing and maintaining a healthy mind and body. The number of spiritual healing centres all over the world have exploded in the last couple of years, as the awakening masses are leaving traditional, chemical based medicine behind. Reiki, crystal, sound and quantum healing, and scalar wave technology is available for those who prefer the energy based healing methods to the traditional chemical pill and surgery solutions.

*Chapter 8*

**HOW I KEEP MY VIBRATION HIGH**

I wrote a whole book to tell *You*, Dear Reader how to keep your vibration high. Now it's time to talk about how *I* do it.

I feel I was born to be a high vibe human. Ever since I can remember I've always been a cheerful person, drawn to people with a similar nature. If I found myself in an unhappy situation I withdrew with my books and lost myself in fairy tales and nature stories. I was one of those people who read fairy tales even as an adult because they usually had happy endings, made me feel good, and allowed me to escape uncomfortable circumstances I was not able to do anything about. I was also drawn to happy, upbeat music and movies, and refused to watch or read sad stories, not to mention listen to miserable, achy-breaky songs.

I never realized the significance of this until well into adulthood when I started noticing how my deepest desires always seemed to come true. Then Arizona happened, and as I began my spiritual journey and started to learn about multidimensionality and how we are creating our reality, I finally realized how my attraction to all things high vibrational had helped form the events of my life. From that point on I had my eyes open. I was aware and conscious, and started experimenting with higher vibrational solutions to my everyday challenges. The results spoke for themselves.

Here is a list of things I do to keep my vibration high:

- I try to wake up every day with a smile and a happy outlook on the day ahead of me. I don't always remember to do it but I try.

- I only listen to, read or watch feel good music, books and movies. I noticed that as my vibration was going higher my tolerance for violent movies lessened. I used to be able to sit around and read while other members of my family were watching movies with guns blazing, people getting tortured and things blowing up. These days I cannot take it. When the blood starts flowing I'm outta there! Well, unless it's Game of Thrones of course.

- I spend time out in nature whenever I can. There is nothing like a walk in a forest, on a mountain path or a beach to put one on a natural "high." It is calming, relaxing and healing.

- I interact with people in a friendly manner. There isn't a sign on anyone's forehead that states 'I'm a friendly person' or 'A**hole here, beware!' Nevertheless, the kind of energy we carry within our energy field is felt by those we interact with. A higher vibrational person is emanating peaceful, friendly energy, and those they come in contact with generally respond in kind. I find that I tend to bump into nice people wherever I go.

- I notice and express appreciation for the good things around me as often as I can, while acknowledging the undesired elements of my environment as well. They don't worry me too much because I know they are only temporary and I have the ability to change them.

- I eat a mostly plant based diet. It's not a requirement, only a personal preference. I know of the terrible ways food animals are treated in factory farms and I don't want to participate in their exploitation.

- I go for walks or bike rides several times a week. Even a 20 minute trip around the block is enough to clear my head, fill my lungs with fresh air and give my heart and muscles a bit of a workout. I forgo the car when running errands in an up to 45 minute walk (one way) radius. This way I end up serving both my mind and body as well as the environment.

- I meditate, although not as often as I'd like. It's important to practice connecting to my inner reality and I love my psychic adventures.

- I record my dreams and psychic experiences so I can examine the connection between my inner world and the outer one.

- I don't judge others or myself. When I do something "wrong" I acknowledge it and move on, trusting that next time I will know better. I don't always do but that's okay, my mistakes are part of my learning experience.

- I do my best to stay away from arguments. They are usually pointless, ego based, and both emotionally and energetically draining.

- When I talk to friends, family or anybody else I steer the conversations towards positive subjects. People complain a lot. In the past I was doing it myself as well, and just like many others I did it out of habit, not really registering that I was doing it. Once I became conscious and aware I began to actually hear the griping coming out of my mouth, and it amazed me how often I caught myself doing it. It took some work to learn to catch it before it "left the building". Now, when I'm conversing with others I move to steer the topic towards a positive outlook as soon as the complaining begins. I still fall back to grumbling once in a while but quickly catch myself and redirect.

- I regularly verbalize my gratitude to the Universe (or to Spirit, Source, or the One Great Consciousness) for my life, for having this incredible Earth experience, for all the support I'm receiving every day of my life, and the opportunity to be here on Earth at such an exciting time to make a difference.

*Chapter 9*

**HOW I CREATE MY REALITY CONSCIOUSLY**

- I spend time to look at the kind of beliefs I hold. They are the pillars of my reality so it's important to make sure that they all serve my highest good. If I encounter a negative experience my first instinct is to ask why I created it, and to see if I can track it back to a past event or an old conditioning that I haven't cleared yet.

- I watch what I'm thinking and listen to what I'm saying at all times. Now that I'm awake I hear instantly when a low vibrational thought enters my head or comes out of my mouth. I acknowledge it in my head, replace it with a high vibrational one and move on.

- I do my best to deal with all negative experiences on the spot. I look at inner reasons I might have drawn them to me for, process them and let them go. I'm very careful about not to let any kind of guilt or resentment fester. I try to process everything as soon as they happen.

- When I'm working on bringing something into my reality I verbalize my intent and affirmations a number of times throughout the process.

- I listen to my gut feelings because I understand that through them I'm being steered towards my goal.

- I always focus on what I want and not the things I don't like, because I know that what I concentrate on is what I'm going to experience. The more I focus on something the more energy I give it, therefore the more it's going to be in my face, be it good or bad.

- I use visualization to draw desired events into my life, to do healing work and to initiate a connection to the non-physical.

- I talk to my cells. Just like everything else in the Universe, my cells have consciousness and they listen to me every second of every day. I regularly thank them for creating this wonderful body for me for this earthly experience. I ask them to correct any imbalances it might have and to work with me to maintain my body's physical well being.

- When I have an idea about something I talk to people who I know will support me. I stay away from the doubters and naysayers and keep my focus on my goal.

- I don't force anything. If there is something in my life I want to change, I set the intention and then sit back and wait to see what happens. For example, one day I loudly stated that I want to become vegetarian and repeated it a few times in the following weeks. A few months later I felt like making myself some veggies while cooking meat for the rest of the family. I started eating less meat and more vegetables, and in a few weeks I found myself almost completely weaned off meat without any cravings or other difficulties. When you force something you create resistance, and resistance keeps you from what you want to achieve.

- I keep an eye on my moods. It's important to do so because I know very well that it is not Life that's supposed to create them, it is my moods that bring about events in my life. Therefore whenever I notice a dark cloud hanging over my head or a negative voice talking in my ear, I quickly shake myself out of it and think of a happy memory, or begin planning something exciting for the future.

- When I'm in a position of urgency or emergency I ask the Universe for help and trust that it comes swiftly. It always does.

- I make an effort to look at the bright side of things and keep a positive, loving attitude at all times. That alone makes a world of difference.

*Chapter 10*

# THE REQUIREMENTS OF LEARNING AND PRACTISING CONSCIOUS REALITY CREATION

### Awareness

In order to create your reality consciously you need to be aware of yourself in the framework of reality. You have to be conscious of your multidimensional nature. You must be able to observe yourself in your everyday life, recognize the source of your low vibrational emotions, thoughts, moods and attitudes and correct them when needed. You have to hear the words coming out of your mouth and be conscious of your beliefs, attitudes, and the actions you take every day. All of that might sound a bit daunting, but tuning yourself to your own thoughts, words and behaviours is just a matter of developing the habit. After a while it will become second nature and you will do it automatically.

## Patience

That's a tough one for many, myself included. The universe is not on the same clock as we are, so anybody who thinks that we can just wave a magic wand, say the words and our dreams will materialize will be greatly disappointed. There is a time lapse between dreaming up something and seeing it come true, and for good reason. Can you imagine the kind of chaos the world would be in if whatever came into our minds would come to pass right away? Thankfully the universe is smarter than letting that happen, so we get enough time for the thoughts to establish themselves in our minds and slowly materialize in good time.

How long the time lapse is between the desire forming and turning into reality depends on many things. Soul contract and karma matters here as well, but how we react to the nudges and opportunities and how strong our focus is play a big part in it. When we are consciously paying attention to and follow our gut feelings instead of talking ourselves out of them we get there faster because we are not taking detours constantly. But even if we do wander off, the universe will always find another way to get you where you want to go and will keep nudging you until you get there. But it will take time. Weeks, months, years, the universe is not in a rush, and it is human nature to get impatient. As they say, the journey itself is no less important - if not more so - than the destination. You learn and experience a lot along the way. One of my reality creations took me 15 years to materialize. It could've been faster of course but I got distracted with life, marriage, immigration and raising a family. I did get there in the end, and the profound feeling of joy and satisfaction upon finally experiencing it happen wasn't any less.

It is different though when there is urgency involved. It has happened to me that I found myself in a 'We-need-help-right-now!' situation, the 'heart-hammering-and-sweating-through-my-blouse' kind, and after I asked the Universe for help I found that it came from an unexpected source very fast. It wasn't me I needed help for, it was someone I was with at the time, and when I saw that he was in trouble I requested assistance. I was worried for this person's well being, and as I was desperately asking for help while pacing the floor with urgency, someone unexpected showed up and he was okay. So please know that you are never, ever alone. You are being watched over, but when in trouble you have to ask for help. The Universe can't get involved if not invited, so you must do your part in bringing relief. In my experience if you do ask help will come. When you are experiencing the intense energy of urgency, panic and heightened level of emotions, the solutions tend to materialize faster, which is something I'm very grateful for.

## Self discipline

As we are all walking different paths at a different pace, some people's awakening is faster than others. Mine is taking a good number of years and it is due partly to my aversion to fast changes. I have always believed that when one experiences radical change (which awakening truly is) the faster the change the more trauma it might cause. So from the very beginning I asked for a gradual, step by step progression in my awakening, so I would have time to integrate all that I was learning and get used to my new world view.

Another reason my awakening is taking such a long time is that I was not always as disciplined as I could've been. I let myself be distracted by a number of things: job, entertainment, family, life in general, and I was doing it all by myself. There was no one around me to do this with, no one to give me a poke when I sat down to surf the net instead of working on my meditation or learning about enlightenment. So I probably could've gotten there faster but I'm here anyway.

We are not on a clock when we are walking the path of awakening. Everyone can take their time, the universe is certainly not in a rush. However, I would recommend using a healthy dose of self discipline to keep at it, meditate, self observe, release, and generally pay attention to the task and not get distracted. The sooner you know what you are doing the easier your life gets, so what's the point of waiting?

## Idealism

What is an idealist? It is a person who sees life not as it is but as he or she wants it to be. Is that *You*, Dear Reader? If not, you'd better prepare to become one because that's what is required when you create your reality consciously. I know what idealists are called by their logical and practical minded peers: dreamers, deluded, impractical. "You see what you want to see" is a common remark, as if it was a bad thing!

Lightworkers were born into this third dimensional world to assist in the Ascension of Earth and everything and everyone on it. We came here to literally change the world, and we will not be doing that by observing 'what is' and going along for the ride. Our task is to awaken in this lifetime, become aware and keep raising our vibration while consciously creating our reality both individually and en masse. The more humans vibrate on a higher frequency and keep creating high vibrational, light filled realities, the faster all low vibrational elements of our existence will fall away and we can rise into the higher dimensions. In order to do that we have to focus on what we want and not what is, because focusing on what is just keeps it in existence longer. To create a future reality, or more precisely, to shift into a more desirable future we have to focus on a probable reality that we want to bring into the present, and for that we need to be idealists. We have to ignore all the doubters and the naysayers, the pragmatists and sometimes even logic, for contemporary logic is a 3D tool that will keep us in the 3D mindset. To be an idealist we have to go where no pragmatist has gone before, and concentrate on the future that we want but has not materialized yet.

## Taking responsibility

When an event that we perceive as negative happens in our life or someone else's, the first reaction most people have is to blame something or someone. To blame is to assign responsibility for our misfortunes to someone or something outside of us, that is to deny the choice we made, which was accepting the negative event as a tool for either learning or teaching others.

When you are creating your reality consciously you know that everything you create comes from within you. That means if you bring undesirable events or people into your life you don't have the luxury of blaming it on anyone or anything other than yourself. You have to take full responsibility for your creations whether they are "good" or "bad." You also have to remember that you came here with a life purpose and contracts with other beings to learn and to teach, so try to find meaning behind every experience and don't waste your time looking for someone or something to blame. Everything happens for a reason, with your agreement, even though you don't remember it. So as they say, when life gives you lemons make some lemonade, and do your best to figure out why *you* presented *yourself* with this opportunity.

## Conviction

Whatever it is that you are creating, it will not go very well if your heart is not in it. It is imperative that you do it all with utter conviction. You cannot create what you want if you don't really believe it's possible or if you don't trust your ability to do it. So you must **know** that what you are working on is going to be realized one day and have no doubts whatsoever. I remind you once again of the importance of keeping the company of supporters around you. If there are none then you do it all by yourself, ignoring all those who doubt and try to dissuade you. You know you can do it; you have the power, the will, the tools, the discipline, and the utter, unshatterable conviction that you will succeed. You need nothing else.

*Chapter 11*

**CO-CREATING WITH THE UNIVERSE**

Just like any film or theatre production, the creation of lifetimes in a physical environment requires teamwork; the cast and crew must work together in order to create a desirable experience. Light beings or higher dimensional consciousnesses who have expressed parts of themselves into physical matter must coordinate their efforts with their non-physical support group in order to successfully navigate their third dimensional reality and create a high vibrational, fulfilling life. What that means is that humans must become conscious in their environment, recognize not just their role in the creation of their reality but also the existence of their invisible team: their Higher Self, Guides and the Universe, and actively work together with them to become the highest version of themselves and their creations.

It took two decades for me to recognize where I stand in the structure of my reality and learn how to do all of this. Today, when I look back in time I can see clearly how my non-physical team led me to that canyon in Arizona where

I got triggered to get on the path of awakening, and how they guided me towards all the information I required on my journey once I expressed my desire for it. How the right books and teachers always appeared when I was searching for knowledge about something specific, how my crown chakra was opened to introduce me to and teach me about my own multidimensional nature, and how my helpers have shown themselves to me so many times, despite that I didn't recognize them because I did not know what I was seeing.

It brings tears to my eyes to realize that I have been respected, accompanied, guided and supported by the Universe (that contains my invisible team) all my life, regardless of me being completely oblivious to it for so long. I was steered, nudged, warned, shown things, and enveloped with love when I cried out in frustration. My team has been with me all this time, and it's hard to believe how slow I was to take notice of their gentle guidance. Once I awakened and became conscious in my reality I worked hard to make up for my previous ignorance. These days I'm fully aware that I'm not walking the path of ascension alone, and it gives me strength, confidence, and warm feelings of appreciation and gratitude.

Many people who are unawakened spend their life on Earth struggling with their existence; feeling like they are on a boat on a stormy sea, being thrown this way and that among the unpredictable waves. Those who become conscious and realize their role in the screenplay of their own life know that there is a reason for everything they experience, and there are no coincidences, only the parts of their creations coming deliberately together to create the events that correspond with their frequency. And when they learn to work together with the Universe and their background team and start creating their reality cooperating with them instead of unconsciously working against them, life becomes so much easier to navigate!

How do we consciously co-create with the Universe? My experience is that we decide what we want to do, let the team know and start working together. Unless there are unreleased energies (negative emotions, trauma, karma) holding us back, our inner guide will continuously steer us towards our goal, while the Universe brings the right circumstances before us. All we have to do is know what we want, pay attention to both the physical and non-physical communications we receive, use the many tools of conscious reality creation that are available to us, trust ourselves, our multidimensional team and the process, and not to be too shy to express our gratitude for our existence and all the help we receive.

*Chapter 12*

## PRACTICAL EXAMPLES AND TIPS FOR CONSCIOUS REALITY CREATION

After studying, experimenting with and practising conscious reality creation for 20 years, I had developed certain methods of creating desired outcomes. Some of these I already talked about shortly in previous chapters. Now I would like to show you a few more simple everyday applications of these methods. All of them are based on my own personal experiences. You can try and experiment with them in your own life and see the results yourself.

Losing weight

I put on a good couple of pounds after my babies were born, so I decided to lose them because I was uncomfortable with carrying around the extra weight. I was used to having a slim body and my bulging midriff didn't do my self esteem any favours. So I made the decision to drop a few pounds and these were the steps I took:

First I chose the number I wanted to reach and set the intent:

*"It is my intent to weigh 120 lbs!"*

To reach that goal I had about 20 lbs to lose. After I set the intent I began to visualize myself standing on a scale, looking at the digital display that showed 120 lbs and being very happy about it. I made myself feel the emotion of it and saw myself jumping with joy and ease, feeling slim, light and full of energy. I repeated this visualization several times a day at first, then few times per week later. In the meantime I verbalized my affirmations regularly:

*"I weigh 120 lbs!"*

Additionally, every time I looked into the mirror I looked past the rolls of fat and "saw" my body slim like it was years before.

In the next few weeks I repeated this process once in a while and waited to see what would happen. I expected that I might lose my appetite or stop craving sweets but none of that happened. Instead, as I was walking around in the mall one day and passed a sport equipment store it came to me that I should buy an exercise bike. It was a strange thought because I never liked them. I always believed in doing my physical activities outside in the fresh air, and having an exercise bike in my apartment seemed a ridiculous idea.

However, I felt such a strong pull that I relented and that's how I began exercising at home. To my great surprise I found that I actually enjoyed it!

A few months went by and my extra weight was coming off nicely, but it seemed that the last few pounds would not budge. I kept doing my visualizations and affirmations hoping I could bike off the rest but it would not go. Then one day I came down with food poisoning, spent the next few days in the bathroom, and by the time I recovered the last rogue pounds had disappeared. As I stood in front of the mirror feeling a bit rough, worn out but happy to be slimmed down, I could not help but laugh at how it worked out. I was reminded once again of how one cannot have expectations about how we get what we want. We ask, and the Universe does its thing in its own way to bring it to us.

## Resolving a conflict

I had an ongoing conflict with a coworker at my workplace for a number of years. For whatever reason we didn't get along, and it was a problem because we worked in close contact every day. I have lost a lot of sleep because of this situation. I felt uncomfortable, bothered and frustrated. Once I became conscious and aware and learned about and understood the concept of 'if you want to change your circumstances you have to change yourself,' I began to experiment with changing the situation. I set the intent to become friendly with each other and began a series of visualizations. I imagined us being nice to each other, chatting and laughing together. I pictured myself giving him a hug every time he walked by, and had imaginary conversations with him where I told him that I forgive him for being mean to me and accept him as he is. It seemed quite a ridiculous exercise in the beginning and felt rather silly but I kept at it for many months, and I was pleasantly surprised when the tension between us actually began to soften. Encouraged by the obvious progress I was making I kept it all going, and after a number of months the years of enmity between us dissolved. Although we never learned to like each other much we became friendly and worked well together, which was good enough for both of us. My goal was not to create a deep, everlasting friendship, but to be able to go to work every day feeling comfortable, unbothered, not having to argue with someone I have to work closely with, and not lose sleep over the things we said to each other.

Now I will tell you something I found incredible at the time, an event that was a real eye opener for me. After things smoothened out between us I had a dream one night in which this coworker and I were hugging and laughing together. I asked him (in the dream) why he was so mean to me and he said that that was his task, and he promised me he would never do it again. As I was recording this dream in my diary I realized what this meant. The conflict situation was a contract between him and myself that we fulfilled, and for that I was immensely grateful. This also gave me the opportunity to be proud of myself for passing this test. Had I not worked to resolve this issue, I would've spent a couple more years at my workplace frustrated and miserable because of our enmity.

So whenever you find yourself around someone who is giving you a hard time, consider the possibility that they are playing out their part of a contract between the two of you, one you both agreed to. This is a test, and being aware of that can be a great help in seeing your situation more clearly and finding a solution to it.

## Creating a dream trip

To create a trip to your favourite destination start, as always, with setting your intent. Verbalize it and name the place you want to go to. Then begin to actively plan the trip. It doesn't matter that you don't have the money for it or don't know whether you are going to be able to take the time off, get the ball rolling. Start looking at pictures of the place, read about its history, visit a travel agency or check travel websites about plane tickets, car rentals, hotel room prices in the area, etc. During meditation visualize your dream destination, picture yourself being there and enjoying the experience. Enhance the visuals with feelings of joy, wonder and excitement. In the meantime do your affirmations several times a week: *"I'm going on a trip to ……."* Keep your focus on your upcoming trip and generate an excited air about yourself every time you think about it. Do your best to discard any and all doubting comments and opinions about your plans. That includes your own, because if you doubt your success you will sabotage your trip. Keep all of this going and keep an eye and an ear open for a nudge, a gut feeling, an idea popping into your head and opportunities presenting themselves. All the while make sure that you live with the utter conviction that you will be there.

I have utilized pretty much all of these reality creation tools (even though unawakened at the time) when I created my 'Big, Impossible Hollywood Dream' that somehow, miraculously, despite the skepticism of everyone around me, turned into reality.

I grew up in Eastern Europe between the '60s and '80s behind the Iron Curtain, where the communist government made travelling to Western countries quite difficult and to America nigh impossible, unless one had family living there. I had a lot of love and enthusiasm for American movies, especially those made by Steven Spielberg. I loved American music, actors, and had a great desire to go see Hollywood where the stars live and movies are made. I dreamed of visiting Universal Studios, driving around in Beverly Hills and meeting my favourite movie star. Considering that I was a teenaged girl living in a communist country my dream was considered quite a far fetched fantasy, and everyone I ever told about it made sure to remind me of that. However, the more I heard from the naysayers the more stubborn I got, and I kept telling them that one day I WILL travel to Hollywood and do all those things I dreamed about. That was the intent setting and verbalizing. I had an old National Geographic magazine with pictures of Hollywood and Universal Studios in it, and those photos fuelled my obsession. I used to sit around and look at them, dwelling on the idea that somehow, someday, I would find myself there. How I was to accomplish that I did not know. I had no money, no relatives in America and seemingly about zero chance to get there. But I persisted. I learned english and read all materials I could find on Los Angeles and the US in general. Then, without me realizing it at the time, events got into motion.

I met a young man I fell in love with and married who had dreams of his own. He did not want to live his life in communism and he dreamed of immigrating to the West to live and raise a family in freedom. Luckily, he had a relative in North America who could help us, and one day we managed to leave our country and headed for a new life in Canada. After a number of years, while we settled down and established ourselves I joined a fan club for my favourite actor, and at one point I flew to Los Angeles to see him perform in a theatre in the company of other fellow fans. After the show we met our star backstage for a Q&A session and took turns having our photograph taken with him.

The day after the performance I went to Universal Studios. I spent the entire day touring the park, enjoying the rides, and standing on a hill, looking over the San Bernardino Mountains and the Jurassic Park ride I toasted Steven Spielberg with a bottle of Coca-Cola. The following morning I took a cab and drove through Beverly Hills on my way to the airport, thus completing my 'Big, Impossible Hollywood Dream.'

## Buying a house

After living in the greater Toronto area for over 30 years my husband and I made the decision to move to a smaller city in northern Ontario. I felt a bit conflicted about the move because I loved my old house even though it was a bit outdated and quite drafty, with an old warhorse of a heating system. I very much liked its layout though, the many windows it had and I loved my garden. The house was missing some things we've always wanted: a garage for example, a good air conditioning system and a nice big shed for the garden tools and other stuff we had. I was hoping that whatever house we found in our new city would have some of those, and would suit us and our needs.

We made the decision a bit late in the season though, and by the time we put our house up for sale and traveled up north to find a new one it was almost September. Most of the houses that were for sale in the spring/summer season were gone, leaving us only a handful to choose from, most of which were not suitable for us. I was quite worried about the situation, so I asked the Universe to help us get a house we would all love and be able to afford. I also set the intention and visualized us finding the right home and put no expectations on what it would look like, only that we would be very happy with it.

A few days later I was looking at the meager offering of listings in the area of our choice, when I noticed that one of the houses that we discarded earlier because we thought it cost too much had lowered its price by a considerable sum. We asked for a viewing, and as we walked inside and around the house we realized that this was the one! It had an almost identical layout to our old house, in fact, it seemed like the updated version of it with a garage, a new heating/cooling system, lots of windows, a spacious heated shed in the back and a south facing backyard where my vegetable garden will get sunshine all day long. So we put in the offer which was accepted and we are still living there today.

Quieting a noisy neighbour

One of my neighbours at my previous house used to play loud music in his car that he was fixing for hours, several times a week. It used to drive me crazy, so when we moved to a new house in a new city I was happy to leave that particular annoyance behind. Imagine my surprise when after a couple of months of blissfully quiet life at the new place we woke up one morning to a loud droning sound. It came from the direction of the neighbour's backyard on our left and it reverberated throughout our bedroom. My husband and I didn't know what to make of it but we shrugged it off, for we thought it was something temporary that we would forget all about in a few hours. That was not the case however. After a short investigation we found that our neighbour gifted his family a hot tub for Christmas that he had installed in his backyard, and the noise came from the pump when it was heating the water. The problem was that it was the middle of winter with the temperatures dipping below -10, -20 Celsius, so the pump was running for hours both during the day and night to keep the water in the tub warm. It was also - quite unfortunately for us - installed on top of a wooden deck, and that meant that the sound rebounded and got amplified, creating a loud, insistent, pervasive noise that left us unable to go to sleep at night until it stopped for an hour or two.

I was lying awake many a nights, wondering why on earth was I creating a noisy neighbour once again. It was quite clear to me that I created this issue for a reason and when we moved to our new place I brought the problem with me. I learned some time ago that when one has this kind of a challenge one cannot just run away from it, for it will remain and persist no matter where we are until either the underlying cause is brought to the surface and worked out or the test is recognized as such and solved.

I have examined my beliefs, attitudes and probable past conditionings and found no reason within myself for manifesting this issue so I decided that it was a test I set for myself, an obstacle I had to overcome. I therefore followed my (by now) usual modus operandi and looked at possible solutions, both the 3D and the high vibe kind. The first thing I did was that I stopped complaining. I knew now that it never helps, it just keeps giving energy to the very issue we are complaining about, making it even more persistent and keeping it right in our faces. As a 3D solution I talked to my neighbour very politely, asking him if he would be kind enough to dampen the sound on his tub in some way so we could sleep, to which he replied that he couldn't and that was that. I wasn't surprised by that, and began my high vibe (or quantum) routine that began with verbalizing the intent:

*"It is my intent to have friendly neighbours and live in a quiet neighbourhood!"*

Once my intent was set I began doing a series of visualizations: opening the windows and listening to the lovely silence of winter, or lying in bed at night and not hearing anything in the bedroom but the soft sounds of sleeping, etc. I also expressed a few verbal requests to the Universe to help me solve my problem, to guide me towards a solution. As I kept imagining my problem solved I also verbalized my affirmations:

*"I love living here with friendly neighbours, and I very much enjoy the peace and quiet that surrounds me day after day!"*

I was doing all of this for literally months. When Spring came and the snow that actually dampened the noise of the tub a bit melted the sound became even louder, so once again I asked my neighbour for his help in solving this problem. As before, he threw up his hands and repeated that he cannot do anything about it. I wasn't discouraged by that because I trusted my methods and knew that there was a solution somewhere, it just hasn't presented itself yet.

During the next few months I kept going with my visualizations and affirmations, and then things began to go my way. One day in July my neighbour told me that he has a group of people coming who will lift and move the hot tub to the other side of his deck so it wouldn't be so close to our house. I thanked him and offered our help with the job, but he did it without us. Once the tub was moved away the situation improved somewhat; the pump was still noisy but now its effect was bearable and we could finally sleep! I was happy with this progress but not completely satisfied, for the noise was still there and I couldn't help but wonder if things just got harder for the people living on the other side of the tub, for it was them who were now getting the full blast of it!

I celebrated this small success but continued my work relentlessly. Visualizations, affirmations, no complaining, and asking the Universe for assistance.

One morning on the third week of September I was clearing the breakfast plates and mugs from the table when I heard a truck idling on the street in front of my neighbour's house. Its engine kept running for some time so I went to the living room window to see what was going on. To my astonishment I saw a flatbed truck with the tub sitting on it, secured by harnesses. I called my husband over to take a look, and together we watched as the truck drove away with the infernal hot tub on it and never came back.

I didn't ask my neighbour why he decided to get rid of it. Whether the people on the other side of his fence complained too or he decided it was not worth the trouble it didn't matter, I was not about to look the gift horse in the mouth. All I cared about was that now I had even more proof that my manifestation methods are working, and I could finally enjoy the peace and quiet I've been missing for the last year and a half. After months of diligent mental and spiritual work I got my quiet life back. So worth it!

## Early retirement

This is my second favourite example after my Hollywood trip, because this one also came together in a way I would've never expected.

As I mentioned before, I grew up in a communist country where the retirement age was 55 for women ever since I could remember. With the fall of the Iron Curtain life very much changed there, and with the new, capitalist system came the extension of required working years. So by the time I turned middle aged the retirement age in my birth country was raised to 62 for women and 65 for men, while in Canada 65 for both sexes. My parents and almost their entire generation had the great fortune of retiring at 55, a dream that is considered unreachable for most of the people in the world today.

I had been working in jobs requiring physical activity all my life, and by the time I was nearing 50 I began to feel some resentment about having to do it for another decade and a half. I was envious of my parents' opportunity to retire so early and wished I could do the same, but with the high cost of living around Toronto I could not imagine how it could be done unless one won the lottery. The thought would not leave me though and I often found myself grumbling about the unfairness of having to work most of our lives, leaving only a few years at the end to enjoy the freedom of not having to do the daily commute and labour. I felt that I deserved so much better than to spend most of my life struggling to make a living and work till I get old. I wanted to do something different, something better, and most of all, I wanted to be free. To wake up when I wanted to, do what I enjoyed and go wherever my feet took me. The thought would not leave me alone but I couldn't figure out a way to do it.

One day I decided to do something about it. I quit grumbling and began my next experiment called 'I'm retiring at 55.' I thought that if this works too, I will have all the proof I wanted that the methods for conscious reality creation are sound, and we are indeed powerful creators with the power to accomplish anything we want in life. So I set the intent, started visualizing, planning things I was going to do when I retired still young, and doing my affirmations. I will never forget how many times I walked up and down on the production floor of the factory I worked at, muttering affirmations under my nose as I was doing my job. This was the affirmation I used:

*"I'm only 55 years old and already retired! I love my life of retirement; not having to go to work every day and enjoying the freedom to do what I want!"*

I was doing this for a few years, quite determined that I would follow in my parents' footsteps and leave the rat race behind while I'm still relatively young. I had brought this up with my family a few times, but any way we looked at it, this dream of mine seemed like an impossible feat to accomplish. Remember though that I have experience with the impossible, and I'm known to annoy my family with my Hollywood story to prove that "impossible" is just a word that means absolutely nothing when one has the skill of conscious reality creation. So I kept at it doggedly with a single minded determination, waiting for signs and directions, whatever the Universe would offer me.

It was about three months after I turned 55 when my older son came home from college one day for Spring Break. He was attending school up north in a small city 700 kms from home and he drove or flew back home for almost every break. He told us how much he enjoyed studying at his school up there, living in a small city with big, open spaces and lots of nature all around with very little traffic, and how much more affordable living is there compared to big cities. He casually mentioned that we would probably like it up there as well, and maybe we could retire there when the time comes.

My husband and I looked at each other and he, being one who shared my desire to retire early sat down with a notepad and pencil and began to do calculations. He sat with it for a while and then told me his results. We spent the next few weeks discussing the possibility of quitting our life where we were living and starting a new chapter up north as a retired couple.

To make a long story short, once the decision was made things happened very quickly. We put the house in order, put it up for sale, sold it in 2 weeks and bought another one in our new city for less than half of what homes cost in the Toronto area. To everyone's astonishment we quit our jobs, packed up the moving van, and up we drove to our new house in our new town and to our new life.

And that is how I ended up retiring at the young age of 55 years and 10 months, following not just in my parents' footsteps but also my great desire for freedom. With the sale of our house and my modest retirement fund we are afforded a small pension that will grow when we officially reach retirement age. In the meantime we can choose whether we want to get a part time job somewhere or just enjoy being retired and do the things we always wanted to do, like writing this book, so I can teach everyone who is interested how to make life into what we want it to be.

## Writing a book

This one is still in progress at the time of writing this book but it's worth mentioning. Ever had the nagging feeling that you were supposed to do something but didn't know what? If the answer is yes then welcome to my life! Or my life as it was before this book was written. During the last seven years I've been tormented with this feeling that I'm waiting for something but don't know what it is. That I'm supposed to do something as well but had no idea what that was either. I talked about it, made videos about it, waited for the proverbial light to come on and illuminate my purpose but nothing happened, except that the nagging feeling persisted. So I did what I always do and started experimenting once again out of sheer frustration. I asked myself: *"What is it that I would like to do? If I could do whatever I wanted right now, if I could name a purpose what would it be?"*

The answer was that I would like to teach. I wanted to teach people all the things I have learned in the past 20 years, after reading all kinds of different spiritual and metaphysical material and putting the picture of reality creation together piece by piece. I had all this knowledge in my head that gave me all of this success and I wanted to help others accomplish the same, because I believed (and still do) that the day we all realize the kind of power we have, will be the day when humanity finally finds freedom.

So there I was with the desire to teach but having no idea how. I was a retired factory worker with a heavy eastern European accent, definitely not an orator, who didn't have the first idea about how to teach. Nevertheless, I set the intention to do it, did some visualizations of teaching and verbalized my affirmation:

*"I am a teacher! I teach people how to create their reality consciously!"*

Then all I could do was wait for the Universe to make its move. I knew it was going to happen, I just didn't know when and how. That is where things stood when the light suddenly turned on.

I was sitting on the couch on a mid-January snowy afternoon, listening to Christmas music and chatting with my husband. I love happy music, and you can't get much happier than singing along with Christmas songs. It was a few weeks after the Holidays but I sing those songs even in the middle of summer so it was nothing out of the ordinary for me. I was doing an online puzzle while humming along with the music, and casually commented that these songs are so great because they make me feel happy inside, therefore keep me in high vibration. The moment those words were out of my mouth I experienced a moment of illumination and suddenly knew what I was supposed to do! I'm going to write a book!

So there was the intent. As always, I verbalized the affirmations, visualized and let myself be led wherever my instinct took me. I sat down to write and the words flowed freely and easily. When I ran out of things to write about I went for a walk where there was no one around me, and verbalized a request to the Universe to help me with some ideas. Then I went home, sat down and wrote a thousand words. Next time I did the same, and once again I came home with new thoughts and ideas for the book.

There were times during this process when I didn't feel like writing anything or working on editing my book so I didn't, especially because the more I got into the formatting part the more complicated it seemed to become.

Therefore I took some breaks from it all and waited for inspiration and instructions. I trusted that I will be guided towards what to do and I was.

And that is where my book writing is today, Dec.16, 2023. I don't know when it will be finished or how, and when it will be published. All I know is that I waited for many years to get to this point and I'm so happy I'm finally doing it! If you are reading this that means that I did finish the book, had it published, and it is helping people live an easier life by teaching them how to create their reality consciously. As a bonus, I also get to record one more success story into my diary!

*Chapter 13*

**COMMON QUESTIONS AMONG THOSE
WALKING THE PATH OF AWAKENING**

Throughout my many years of visiting spiritual and metaphysical websites, Facebook groups and forums, I have encountered a number of questions that seem to pop up everywhere. Here are a few of the most common ones I feel I can answer based on my research and experiences:

Q: *There is all kinds of spiritual information out there. How do I know which ones to listen to?*

A: You listen to the ones you resonate with. As you start your spiritual journey you will find yourself attracted to certain kinds of information, while others you reject because they don't feel right. If something doesn't "speak to you" that means it's not for you.

"But how is that possible?" you ask, "Aren't we, spiritual people all on the same path, meaning that we all need the same information?"

We may be on the same path, but remember that we are not all on the same frequency and we don't all come from the same background. The kind of information people are attracted to reflects their level of vibration. I learned that as I progressed throughout my own journey. Looking back, I can see now how I went from "spiritual kindergarten" to "university," always drawn to material that was on the level of my vibration. I even noticed myself skipping a few "classes" because as I awakened and started to consciously create my reality my vibration shot up, and some of the material became too outdated for me to get into.

There is also our background and our old belief systems that greatly influence the kind of spiritual information we accept. For example, I came from scientific interests and never wanted to have anything to do with religion. That is why every time I came across spiritual information with the word 'God' in it I ran the other way. Thankfully we have many kinds of spiritual teachers teaching people of all backgrounds, so everyone can find the material that suits them, information they resonate with. As we progress we keep moving on to new teachers and new ideas that match our vibration at the time, until eventually we feel that we don't need teachers anymore.

Q: *My friends and family think I'm weird and they are not interested in spirituality at all. What can I do to change their mind?*

A: Nothing. I'm guessing that's not what you want to hear but there is really nothing to do. People's beliefs are what they are, it's theirs, just like your beliefs are yours. You would not want someone to try to convince you to accept their beliefs, and if those around you are not open to yours then you have to let it go. People walk their own path and it doesn't have to be the same one as yours.

Not everyone will awaken in this lifetime. Others might still have learning to do, challenges to overcome and contracts to fulfill, and you have to let them enjoy their own play, after all that is why they were born into physical reality. We can influence others by our awakening and speaking about our own beliefs, but we cannot force anyone to join us when they are not ready.

Q: *Does awakening have any downsides?*

A: It sure does but they are temporary. Awakening and becoming conscious is not an easy process for many, myself included. As exciting as finding out that you are so much more than what you always thought yourself to be is, it can also be pretty confusing, especially if you are new to the spiritual side of life. At first you can get a bit lost in all the information out there, and it can take some time to sort yourself out and see what fits and what doesn't. As you are changing you might lose some people around you, and find yourself lonely and often unable to relate to people you used to be comfortable being around before. As your worldview changes and you turn inward you find that you no longer have much interest in world events, political intrigues, family dramas or even your usual type of entertainment. When you meet people you often don't know what to talk about because small talk no longer satisfies you. You might feel that life as it is becomes boring, it no longer suits you, and you dream of something better but don't quite know what.

As I was awakening I went through a lot of that. At one point I found myself feeling like I was trapped in a video game on Level 1 where I have done all the challenges, and now I was desperately waiting to get to Level 2 so I could get going.

Awakening is quite the journey, and at one point you realize that you are no longer the same person you were before. Your life is also no longer what it was before. There is a sense of loss for a while but what follows is hope and excitement, for you are entering a new frontier, a new adventure, a new way of seeing and being that you feel is right and good and empowering. So work at it, because the journey may be hard but the results will make it all worthwhile. Becoming conscious will change your life forever because you will finally be able to move forward.

Awakening can also test one's patience. Some people awaken pretty quickly, for others it takes a long time. My awakening came in stages: first there was the "Oh wow!" period, the newness, the wonder and amazement as I found out that I was so much more than just flesh and blood, then came the excitement, the feverish research and consumption of spiritual and metaphysical information, and the experimentation with my newfound abilities. All that was followed by years of silence as all that knowledge settled down in my mind, my worldview shifted and I wondered what would come next. It was a frustrating period because I found that I have outgrown the life I knew before, but did not yet know what I was supposed to do in the new one. It took a number of years for me to figure it out. Now my book is written, I'm waiting to see how it's going to get published, so once again I've hit the next 'what now?' period. I think it's a safe bet that in a while things will swing into action again, and I will look back at these quiet times and have a laugh at my impatience.

So be prepared, if you are a slow awakener like me your patience will be tested. The universe is not in a rush, it takes its sweet time, so go with the flow my friend and enjoy the ride. I certainly am.

Q: *I have a hard time taking in the concept of living multiple lives at the same time.*

A: For those on the path of awakening the concepts of multidimensionality and non-linear time can be quite a mind bender. I have struggled with them myself for some time, until finally I was able to create a picture in my mind that made sense.

Imagine a tree full of leaves on its many branches. That tree is *You*. You are experiencing being a tree one leaf at a time. Every individual leaf is *You*, and you live your lives from being a bud through growing into a full leaf, then slowly turn yellow, die and fall off the tree. The individual leaves are all connected through the stems, branches and the sap inside the tree, but they are unaware of this and all think of themselves as being separate from the rest of the tree. Through your existence as a tree you experience being leaves on the sunny side of the tree and the ones in the shade. In some of your lives as a leaf you are green and healthy, in others yellowed and curled or slowly eaten by insects. Through experiencing the lives of all the leaves you will know what it's like to be a tree. At one point you begin to wake up, see the other leaves around you and recognize them as *You*, and you will know that you have been the whole tree the whole time.

Q: *I'm walking the path of awakening and find myself all alone, both physically and spiritually.*

A: Welcome to the club! The world is full of awakening people who suddenly find themselves different from everyone else and alone in their new state of mind. I have also found myself in the same situation when I began my journey, but soon picked up companionship along the way. Thanks to the internet I found a great number of online forums full of both newbies like me and more experienced and knowledgeable people, who shared my feelings of loneliness and could teach me or point me in the direction of helpful information. I developed online friendships that lasted years, and always had someone I could turn to when I needed advice or just a few minutes of spiritual conversation. Today, with the explosion of Facebook groups and Youtube channels you can find companionship everywhere, you just have to look.

They say that the spiritual path is a lonely one, and it is true because everyone's journey is unique. There are similarities with others, but no two people are born with exactly the same purpose, challenges or level of vibration. No two develop the same background during their journey. All of us do it in our own individual way and reach different levels at different times. Even within a spiritual community we are all unique.

As a lightworker I sometimes felt alone and spiritually unsupported during my awakening. There were times when

I got angry and frustrated because it rankled that I was here on a "mission" to assist humanity's ascension on my own, and I had to struggle so much. One day during a rather trying day at work the proverbial cup runneth over, and I couldn't help unleashing a rather emotional and colourful diatribe at Spirit, Source, the Universe, my Guides, or whoever was listening. I threw up my hands and loudly expressed my displeasure with all this "spiritual bullshit" that we are never alone and such, and asked why on earth do I have to work so hard and struggle to make a living, why isn't life easier, how can I help others when my life is consumed with working to survive and raise a family and just generally trying to make it. I didn't intend to be mean and accusatory, it is not my nature, but I've just so had it with the struggle!

Once I ran out of angry words I stopped to catch my breath, and suddenly I was flooded with LOVE. I call it that because I can find no other word to describe it; it was an emotion that fully enveloped my entire being and filled me with feelings of …well, the words love, care and belonging comes the closest. It was such a strong and overwhelming emotion that my heart felt full to bursting, my eyes filled with tears, I was almost choking with it. I just stood there with tears streaming down my face and tried swallowing some of them as this incredible feeling took me over completely, and then I suddenly knew. I knew with utter certainty that no matter how hard life is, how much we struggle or even suffer we are never alone, and I was being shown exactly that.

I have seen another proof of this much later, at a time when I specifically asked for it. I went for a walk on a snowy morning, enjoying the look and feel of winter at its best; thick snow blanketing the ground that dampened all sounds, the cold fresh air and large falling snowflakes gently hitting my face as I walked. I trekked into the small forest near my home, and when I reached the river I stood on the shore and spoke to Spirit. I thanked my ancestors for preparing the ground for my life experience, Source for my existence and the life of freedom I now enjoy, my helpers for being there for me when I ask for it, my cells for creating this strong and healthy body for me, and all my fellow light beings who are and have been acting out the personalities who participated in my life in various roles to help me in my development. At the end of expressing my gratitude I asked my guides if they could show themselves to me because I would love to see them, and requested that they would appear to me in a way that I would recognize them. I stood around for a few minutes, feeling a little bit silly but nothing happened, so I shrugged and headed out of the forest. About halfway on the way home, as I was admiring the look of the snow covered landscape I suddenly found myself surrounded by a miriad of tiny spots of dancing lights. They were shimmering around me, and I was amazed to realize that these little pinpoints of lights were the ones I used to see regularly when I began my awakening journey over two decades ago! I never knew what they were, they disappeared after a few years and I missed them ever since. Now, as I was seeing them again I laughed out loud in recognition and joy, watching them happily dancing around me. I thanked them for showing themselves to me once again, and after a few seconds they disappeared.

As the years went by I also experienced other kinds of events that clearly indicated to me that we are being helped from "beyond." One day I went shopping and as I was coming out of the store the theft alarm sounded. I had nothing with me with any kind of security tag and no one came to stop and search me so I just kept going to my car and drove away. Or I would've, except as I slowly turned out of the parking lot a car appeared from my right and I bumped into it. After the fender bender as I was driving home I wondered how did I not see the car coming. At the same time the memory of the theft alarm flashed through my mind, and it occurred to me that I was given a warning about something that was coming.

At another time I was wasting some time on Youtube, watching stupid stuff to entertain myself. I found a bunch of videos where scammers were running at or laying down in front of cars to claim insurance money. Yes I know, it was not exactly high vibe entertainment but back then I didn't know any better. The videos were both revolting and hilarious and I watched quite a few of them, clicking on one video after the other. After about a half an hour of this the phone rang. I picked it up and it was a wrong number. I went back to my stupid videos and continued watching them when the phone went off again. This time it was a telemarketer and I quickly hung up. I clicked on the next scammer video and started watching the next set of fools throwing themselves in front of slowly rolling vehicles, when you guessed, the phone rang again! I knew by then that something was up but I picked up the phone anyway, and this time it was a duct cleaning company offering me services. I thanked them for the offer and slowly hung up the phone. I sat around for a bit, wondering what was going on but nothing popped into my head, so I searched for the next batch of silly videos and started watching them. When I heard the sound of the phone ringing for the fourth time I had my answer. "Okay, okay, I'm stopping!" I yelled and turned YouTube off. I didn't even bother picking up the phone for I knew there was no point. I got the message loud and clear.

There is even more proof that we are not alone in our everyday life. I cannot count the number of times when it happens that I'm sitting around reading a book, solving a puzzle or watching TV, when I feel like someone is playing with my hair. It's sort of a light buzzing or electric sensation that I have felt in my hair, on the tip of my nose (I just smiled because my dad's face just popped into my mind, he used to play with my nose when I was a child) or the side of my face. For a long time I didn't know what this was but now I'm aware, and whenever it happens I smile, think *"Thank you!"* and call out to my husband: "Hey, someone is messing with my hair again!"

So believe me, your path may seem lonely and sometimes you might feel unsupported but you are never truly alone, you only have the impression of it. You are surrounded by invisible supporters from the day you are born, loved ones who are no longer with you physically but come to you to show their love, and helpers who are ready to give you a hand *whenever you ask for it*. The only question is whether you are paying attention to it.

Q: *I'm saddened by the state of the world today. What can I do to make it better?*

A: Raise your vibration as high as you can. Your immediate environment always reflects the level of your frequency. If you master the skill of living in high vibration you will see how much better your life is going to become. There are probable realities running alongside this one, and you will always shift into the appropriate one based on the frequency you vibrate with. It works both individually and en masse. If everyone on Earth lived high vibrational lives and humanity gave off a mass high frequency there would be no opportunity for wars, lack, poverty, disease and misery to sneak into our lives. The human race is awakening together. We are sitting in the middle of a great shift, heading towards what in spiritual circles we call an

Ascension, the rising up to higher frequencies to the higher dimensions. When humanity raises its vibration it will shift into a reality that matches its frequency, and that is how we will change the world.

I had difficulties understanding this concept until one day I found it beautifully explained by one of my beloved teachers. To paraphrase Bashar, we don't change the world we are on, we just shift to another Earth with people and events that reflect the vibrational shift we have made in ourselves. The way I understand his words is that the world we shifted from is still there, we are just not on it anymore because it does not correspond with our present frequency, therefore our consciousness is no longer focused there. According to him there are many versions of Earth with different levels of vibration, and some of them already destroyed themselves.

So at the end of the day it is this "simple": if you don't like what you see around you change your vibration, and you will shift into a reality that matches it. We are creating both individual and the mass reality together, and many people are vibrating on low frequencies. Therefore at this point you will see both good things around yourself and ugly things out in the world. Once the rest of humanity catches up though... I can't wait to see that!

There is another way to make the world a better place, though one that is not too popular with a lot of people: send light, loving energy to the baddies of the world. I'm talking about dictators, murderers, thieves and all manner of people who make others' life miserable.

Why them? Because these people operate on a very low level of vibration, that is why they are committing atrocities and crimes against humanity. They live in darkness, therefore they are the ones who need the light the most. So send them love and healing energy to help raise them out of their darkness to a higher frequency. But first and foremost you must take good care of your own energy and frequency. Be the best version of yourself and that will attract the best version of the world to you, that is how you make a difference.

Q: *Why are people hurting each other? So many fall victim to robbers, murderers, abusers, pedophiles, wars, etc.*

A: Once you understand the concept of multi-dimensionality and recognize the "play" we have written for ourselves with us in the lead and all the supporting players we made contracts with, you will realize that there are really no victims here, only agreements being fulfilled. The participants wanted to experience certain life situations, so some beings volunteered to be the perpetrators and others their "victims." The challenge is whether the actors would awaken from the play and resolve the issues by way of forgiveness and letting go, or remain asleep and live their entire life with the trauma never released. Then once the play is finished the participants may choose to be born again to improve their performance and finish their task, or to switch roles so that in the next incarnation they can be victims or perpetrators too.

When you look at Creation from outside of the limiting view of the third dimensional matrix you will see that the intent of these hurtful, often horrendous interactions between humans is education. Light beings such as you, me and all of us keep incarnating in 3D to experience, learn, teach and understand ourselves. From the unawakened human's point of view it is a tragedy that there is so much pain and suffering we cause each other and it's difficult to accept that we do it as lessons for ourselves, but understanding will come as we are becoming more and more conscious.

Look at it this way: if you were an actor in a war movie who has forgotten that he is in a film, playing the role of a soldier defending his country and being shot at, you would be scared, horrified, hurt and traumatized right up to the point where you woke up and realized that it's just a movie! And then chances are you would want to switch and play the bad guy too because you don't know what it's like, and you'd want to experience and understand that point of view as well. So you go back into the movie, forget that you are an actor, and play the aggressor until you wake up again or there is a resolution of some kind.

"What is the point?" you may ask.

The point is that you need to know war in order to appreciate peace and experience hate to understand the significance of love. That is why these contracts with other light beings are so important; they are our teachers in our quest to receive the lessons we came here to learn.

*Q: Can we communicate with our loved ones who passed on already?*

A: We sure can. There are psychics who've been able to communicate with the dead ever since they were born. Some of them are so good at it they can make a living out of it. However, the vast majority of people - myself included - don't have the talent to contact those who are not with us anymore, at least not purposely, any time we wish. That doesn't mean there is no communication between us, for even though we may not know how to contact them they do know how to find us when we are in an altered state of consciousness, either during meditation or in our sleep.

Not long after losing his grandmother to old age, I woke up to find my husband looking thoughtful while sitting up in bed one morning. I asked him if he was all right and he told me that he had a wonderful dream, in which he had a long conversation with his grandmother about all kinds of things. My husband was never really close to her and as an adult he had some issues concerning her role in some family matters, but he mourned her when she passed for they loved each other. In this dream they talked about much and more, and upon awakening he felt warm and loved as if the weight of unresolved issues have been taken off his shoulders. He marvelled at the sensation and smiled about the memory, but when I told him that this was a real event where his grandmother said good bye to him and cleared the energies between them he remained skeptical. "It was just a dream," he said, and I left it at that.

A decade and a half later my own father died in his mid-seventies, and we travelled home for his funeral and to take care of his estate. One of the items we had to look for was his bankbook. It contained all his banking information, his accounts and the balances on them. While alive he took care to show us where he kept the book, so in the case of his passing we would know where to find it. Naturally, when we looked for it in the place he showed us it wasn't there. We searched his whole apartment and couldn't find it.

A few nights later he came to me in my dream. He was dressed in his grey trousers and blueish-green shirt, the way I've seen him so many times in the past many years. He looked to be in his fifties, his full head of hair all grey that made him look so handsome in my eyes. Being as practical in the afterlife as ever he told me where his bankbook was. We talked about other things as well but I could not recall them in the morning. I remembered his love and felt happy because there were no unresolved issues between us, I have already dealt with those during my clearing sessions.

Upon awakening I couldn't help but laugh a little as I told my husband and other members of my family about my dream. We went to his common law spouse's place where he spent the majority of his last years, that's where he indicated his bankbook now was and we quickly found it. My husband was all amazed, and I took this opportunity to remind him of his conversation with his deceased grandmother fifteen years before. In this new light he was willing to entertain the idea that the communication from her was actually real.

I would bet good money that there are a great number of people with similar stories everywhere. Some of them write it off as "Oh, it was just a dream," but others understand that they have experienced a real conversation with their loved ones, and feel that a release of energies have taken place during the non-physical encounter.

Q: *What about demons, ghosts, negative entities, etc.?*

A: I'm happy to say that I have not much experience with them. As I mentioned before, I was born with a high vibration enough that I have never really had to deal with any of that. I believe that negative entities of any kind cannot be around you once your vibration takes you out of their reach. They are low frequency beings attracted to low vibrational people.

Since our beliefs are very much part of the building blocks of our reality, if you experience negative energies around you for example and you follow the old traditions and smudge, it will probably work for you just like it worked for our natives and other ancestors. I dare you though to take it one step further and use a higher solution: raise your vibration! Once you are out of reach for all lower vibrational entities you will need no smudging or any other kind of protective rituals and ceremonies. Your high frequency will attract only matching entities, events and people.

But if you are dealing with encounters with lower vibrational entities, psychic attacks and the like, remember that you create your reality and within that framework you are the boss! You can order these unwanted visitors away with clear statements about them not being welcome in your life. Send them love and direct them to go either back to their own domain or into the light. Work on raising your vibration so they will not be able to attach themselves to you.

A lot of people in the spiritual community talk about the need for protective chants, talismans, crystals, visualizations, rituals and ceremonies. I have never been comfortable with those because asking for protection suggests that I'm not safe in some way and I have never felt that. Again, I want to remind the reader that *You create your reality, every aspect of it, based on your thoughts, beliefs, attitudes, or in other words, your vibration.* If you believe that you are not safe and you need to protect yourself then that is the reality you are going to create. So beware of participating in mass beliefs that don't serve your highest good. I know they are popular but you don't have to partake. Just watch your vibration!

Q: *Wouldn't it be cool if we could build a time machine and go back and forth in time?*

A: What do you need a time machine for? Your consciousness is all you need to visit other times and realities. You do it all the time, either consciously or unconsciously in your dreams, during meditation, through past life regression, etc.

You know that we live in a multiverse and time is not linear. It just seems so from our limited 3D point of view. All the "past" and probable "future" realities are existing in the quantum field and you can access them in an altered state of consciousness. Imagine that all those multi-dimensional realities are TV stations and you can use your consciousness to tune into whichever one you wish to see. All those channels are running at the same time, but you see only the one you are tuned into. I have not developed the skill to do it on demand, but I sometimes randomly tune into these other realities while meditating or dreaming.

There are people who can access the quantum field (or Akashic Records) regularly by having excellent control of the process. If you are like me and you are not one of those people then work on remembering your dreams, keep a diary and record your experiences both during dreaming and meditation.

One day during a meditation session I found myself standing on a street corner, just outside of a parking lot. As I stood there I watched a number of old style, pastel coloured cars passing on the street. One of them, a light green car that reminded me of a very "old" Citroen turned into the parking lot right where I was standing. It was a scene straight out of the 50's or 60's in western Europe. I had no doubt that was what I was seeing.

At another time I was walking on a dirt path in a jungle with a rock wall on one side. There were figures carved into the rocks, the same kind you see when you visit the tourist sights of Mexico and its surrounding countries. The difference was that these carvings were new! I wish I had the mind to look down and see what I was wearing, but these snippets of images rarely lasted longer than a few seconds and I was too busy looking at the carved rock to remember that I should take a look at myself as well. Anyway, that is time travel for you, two of the few I had the great fortune to experience. No time machine required!

Q: *I'd like to remember my past lives. What do I have to do?*

A: There are people who can access this information fairly easily, but unfortunately, just like most people on the planet, I'm not one of them. So if we want to know what kind of lives we've been experiencing on Earth we have to investigate. Aside from dream recall, meditation and past life regression, one reliable method I found during my years of experimenting was self observation. Yes, I know, that sounds too simple, but I tell you it works! All you have to do is observe your interests and your emotional reactions to situations, objects, your surroundings and experiences.

I have always been interested in ancient civilizations, especially Egypt, the Mayans and the North American native tribes. I have been reading about them since elementary school, but I could never figure out the reason for my avid interest until I started awakening and learned about reincarnation, past lives and past life memories. My connection to these ancient times have been confirmed by my psychic experiences, dreams, a quantum hypnosis session and my reaction to certain objects and environments.

For example, my lifelong interest in the natives of North America suggested a past life (or more lives) in one or more of the tribes. It's been confirmed by my experience in Canyon de Chelly, Arizona, and during a QHHT session where I experienced being a native child, a young and an old woman living in a tribe. My attraction to the ancient Mayan ruins and their culture indicated another past experience, which was confirmed by my vision of walking in the jungle and looking at stone carvings during a meditation, and the sensations of love and feeling at home when I visited some of the ruins in Mexico.

If we are talking about lifelong interests I have to mention my passion for the underwater world most of my life, especially in my youth. I used to be glued to the TV every time a nature program would show the life of plants and creatures in all the waters of our planet, great and small. My connection to this world was proven by several dreams in which once I was a fish, hiding from a predator in a small hole, other times a dolphin and an orca, one freely swimming in the ocean, the other living in captivity at an entertainment centre.

The plight of the Jews during the Holocaust has also been a longtime interest of mine; I have read many books and watched numerous documentaries about it. I also had a fascination with their language and wondered what it would be like to be able to speak it. Back in the early 2000s during a drive through Germany I had the opportunity to visit one of the most infamous concentration camps in Dachau with my family. It was a somber place just as I thought it would be, and it gave me the answer to what I've been wondering about for many years: "*Did I have a life as a Jew during the Holocaust?*" It would certainly explain my fascination with the event and their language, and my strong dislike of the sound of the German language that always mystified me.

We were walking around in the camp, exploring the remains of the barracks where the prisoners were housed, and looking at the many objects and photographs exhibited in the museum. When we got to the gas chambers I walked in myself, stood next to the wall and mentally asked: *"Have I been here before?"*

The answer came swiftly, as suddenly there was an electric buzzing sensation on the back of my head. It was quite strong and unmistakable, and lasted for almost a minute. I smiled, closed my eyes, sent a wave of love and healing energy towards the (my?) spirit and wordlessly expressed my gratitude for the confirmation.

Another interesting example is my fear of bears that I could never explain; the bear-chasing-me kind of nightmares I have had since childhood, and the literal fear I felt every time I was hiking in the woods despite that I never had any encounters with bears of any kind. This made me wonder if I experienced a bear related misfortune in one of my past lives, which was confirmed during one of my quantum hypnosis sessions where I saw a bear coming at me.

You see, it is this simple: observe yourself and watch your reactions. Have you ever felt upon visiting a place for the first time that you know this place and you are at home? Ever had an unexplained interest in something, or a fear, a phobia, a strong reaction to something or someone?

These are all clues that indicate a previous life experience stored in your subconscious. There is a good reason why some people are afraid of heights, water, fire, confined spaces, etc. During past life regression sessions people with those kind of phobias have talked about falling, drowning, burning and being stuck in a dark place in a so called previous life. So if you pay attention to your feelings and reactions in certain situations you will get an idea about your experiences in some of your other incarnations.

I have a number of unconfirmed theories about some of my past lives based on certain reactions I experienced in my past: my deep attraction to anything Egyptian, the feeling of being at home not just in Arizona and Mexico but also in New York City, and a strong emotional reaction I had to the sight of a Douglas DC-3 aircraft in an aviation museum. All of these are indications of other lives I lived and experiences I had stored in my subconscious.

Your reactions to many things give you hints of who you are or have been in other lifetimes, all you have to do is pay attention to them.

One great way I used to catch glimpses into who I was/am in another life was giving myself instructions at bedtime and recall the dream in the morning. Before I went to sleep at night I verbalized my intent:

*"It is my intent to look into a mirror in my dream and see myself in other lifetimes, and to remember it in the morning!"*

Thanks to this method I have discovered several other *Me*s existing in other realities. All of them were female although different ages, races and nationalities. One of them was a forty-ish looking woman with shoulder long, coloured, brown wavy hair, living in a city that looked to be in France or a similar European country, an another one was young and had oriental features.

The most memorable one of them was an old lady in her seventies who was at a health clinic. In the dream I was her and I was sitting in the doctor's office, talking to the physician about my health issues. At one point I stood up and went to the hand basin, and while I washed my hands I looked up into the mirror above the counter. An older lady looked back at me with plain features and short, dark strawberry coloured, curled hair. While I was looking at "my" image I knew I was looking at myself, despite that "I" looked nothing like me. When I awoke in the morning I recalled the dream and the face I saw in the mirror very clearly, and promptly registered the event in my dream diary.

Q: *How do UFOs and ETs fit into all this?*

A: They fit in very well, for ETs are not as "alien" as you might think. They are us in different incarnations. When we established that we live in the multiverse in many vibrational levels of realities it didn't just mean Earth. The multiverse contains an infinite number of Earths and other planets, and we have focuses or lives on many of them on different levels of vibration. The aliens are us in a different kind of "bodysuit," experiencing a different kind and level of existence. Some of them are here to keep an eye on our development as a species. They (or should I say 'we'?) have been here ever since this holographic matrix has been created to experience physical reality. We have been observed all this time and allowed to play out our adventures and experiences as per our agreement before we were born.

A lot of people wonder why we can't see them up in the sky or walking among us except for the rare sightings. To answer that we have to remember that the third dimensional reality we live in is a very low vibrational environment, and those observing us are high frequency consciousnesses, capable of consciously manipulating energy and matter on a much higher level than we are. Our physical body is visible because our atoms and molecules are vibrating slowly, thus creating a dense material for the body that houses our consciousness. Theirs is a high frequency one, therefore invisible to the eyes of a 3D person.

To explain that let's imagine a cooling fan for example. When the blades are stationary or spinning on a slow speed you can see them clearly, but once you turn the fan on a high setting the blades will spin so fast that they become invisible to the naked eye. A high frequency craft or being can hover above you or stand right next to you and you will not see either, because 3D people with 3D consciousness will see only the objects that correspond with their level of vibration. So to be able to see an alien craft in the sky or beings on the ground, either we have to raise our frequency or they have to lower theirs.

As humanity raises its frequency en masse, beings, objects and phenomena of higher vibrational nature will be visible for us to see and that is when physical contact can be made. Until then, we can connect to them via our consciousness through meditations and dreams, and that is being done by a number of higher vibrational people all the time. We call many of them channels, channelers or mediums.

Communication with aliens - or in other words our other selves in higher frequency realities on other planets - is done all the time by people all over the Earth. Some channel them publicly, while others do it privately in altered states of consciousness through meditation or automatic writing. This activity used to be believed to be for the few "chosen ones," but as more and more people are waking up to their true nature and learn to access the multidimensional part of their being, channeling and recognizing their other than Earth bound existences have become more widespread in the spiritual community.


Q: *Who are the 'lightworkers?'*

A: The term 'lightworker' is rather well known in spiritual and metaphysical circles, and represents a large number of higher vibrational beings born into this 3D world in order to assist Earth and humanity to raise their vibration, and therefore their frequency. As we are on our way to higher dimensions, Earth and all her people need all the help we can get to pull ourselves out of the lower vibrations: the darkness, the mindlessness and the never-ending struggle of the third dimensional reality we've been playing around in for thousands of years.

The lightworkers of our present time have began arriving in great numbers from around the '50s and '60s. Dolores Cannon, the well known American hypnotist, developer of the quantum hypnosis healing therapy (QHHT) called them the 'Three Waves of Volunteers' because their mission is voluntary. They come into this world with a high vibration, maintain it throughout their lifetime as well as they can and spread it wherever they go, some of them knowingly, others unconsciously, because they are affected by the amnesia of the 3D existence like everyone else. Today there are millions of lightworkers living on Earth, doing their work quietly or not so quietly, diligently raising the vibration of humanity. Many of them remain unaware of their nature either all their life, or until they are activated to wake up like the way I was. I had not known about any of this until I got the wake up call and began my journey of self discovery, but my subconscious did know because it kept me on the high vibe road throughout a somewhat turbulent child and early adulthood.

Lightworkers who are unaware of their nature go about their lives spreading their high vibrational energy unknowingly. They are people who open the doors for you and smile at you without any apparent reason. They dream about changing the world to one where everyone is well fed and clothed, have a roof over their heads and where dreams always come true. They do this instinctively, without being aware of the power of their energy.

Being a lightworker doesn't mean high vibing and flying on clouds all the time. They have their own challenges and ups and downs, they can drop into low vibrations like everyone else and get bogged down by the trials of everyday life. Many lightworkers struggle with the low vibrations of this world and feelings of being alone and not belonging here. Some describe a certain level of homesickness for a place they don't remember. Those that awaken have their own challenges: from unexpected and unexplained psychic experiences to becoming detached and alienated within their own friend and family circles, and the transformation of their entire inner and outer world. It takes a while to go through the journey of awakening, absorbing a great deal of information and experience, make sense of all of it, and learn to apply the knowledge gained in one's everyday life.

Conscious lightworkers are set to raising Earth and her people's vibration deliberately. They work and keep an eye on their own frequency, go where other people are to assist, teach, heal or positively affect those around them in any way they can. They share their knowledge, send energy to others, and participate in mass meditations. They are here to make a difference: to help awakening others and raise and keep our frequency high, so we can ascend to the higher dimensions.

Q: *There is a lot of controversy about meat versus plant based diet. Should all spiritual people be vegans or vegetarians or it's okay to eat meat?*

A: My personal take is that there is no such thing as "should" when one is on a personal spiritual journey. Your feelings, opinions and actions are always reflections of the present level of your frequency. The higher your vibration the more you will want to move away from anything with negative energy.

Animals in general are high vibrational beings, but those in captivity, bred for human consumption and raised on factory farms are living short but miserable lives, suffering greatly. Their feed is polluted with unnatural ingredients, the structure of their bodies is manipulated and their living circumstances are unspeakable. They live a hard life without being exposed to any love, care and compassion, and die full of fear and pain. That kind of existence creates a great deal of low vibrational energy. The question is whether you are willing to bring that into your body or not. To answer that, you have to listen to yourself and no one else. You have to determine what your feelings are; are you okay with it or does it bother you? Do you think the meat is good for you or not?

When I was a child I didn't like meat. Not because I was worried about the animals' welfare, food animals were raised on pastures with love and care where I came from, so that wasn't an issue. I simply wasn't a meat eater by nature. I preferred grain based foods and fruits and vegetables. My parents and grandparents didn't accept that and insisted that I ate what they did, and after a while I got used to the taste of meat. I was a meat eater for a very long time, well into my awakening years. But at one point, when I reached a certain level of vibration I simply felt that I did not wish to eat meat anymore. So I set my intention to switch to a plant based diet and that was it.

There is no right or wrong about what you take into your body and into your mind, it's all a matter of choice.

Depending on your beliefs and/or your level of vibration you will consume whatever feels right for you at that time of your spiritual development.

There is also an important element of our existence that I don't see too many people talking about and that is transmutation. As multidimensional spiritual beings we have the ability to transmute energy. We actually do this all the time without even being consciously aware of it; we go into a low vibrational situation and through our higher vibration transmute it to match our frequency.

If you like meat but worry about consuming the low vibrational energy it carries you can transmute it by giving it a blessing. You can visualize thanking the animals for giving their lives for us and appreciating their sacrifice to sustain our bodies. Our ancestors used to do this regularly through prayers and ceremonies. Unfortunately we have discarded and forgotten these traditions that allowed us to live together with nature in balance.

At the end of the day you eat whatever you feel you want to. My experience is that as your frequency is rising your preferences will change to match your level of vibration. Listen to your heart and do what feels right. You will know what to do.

Q: *How do I know I have issues to heal and release?*

A: You will know by observing yourself. When you pay attention to your thoughts, actions, reactions and your instincts, notice the signals your body and your mind are giving you. When you take time to remember and record your dreams you will see the hints you are being given by your non-physical Self (the Higher Self). When you notice yourself getting triggered by or have negative attitude towards certain things, you know that there is an issue there. When you experience certain ailments they are indications of underlying emotional issues. I know people who have been greatly limited in life and felt immobilized by their circumstances, who have been dealing with mobility issues most of their life. Another person who's retired from active work has been dreaming about a certain work situation night after night, years after his retirement, which is a clear indication that there is an issue there that he needs to process and release or the dreams will keep plaguing him.

At the end it all comes down to how well you know yourself and whether you are willing to put in the effort to dig deeper and explore all that is within you. Your Higher Self gives you plenty of hints and nudges, you just have to notice and understand them and work your issues out. That may sound a bit daunting but with practice it gets easier.

*Q: I'm living a hard life. I've been struggling with abuse, addictions and toxic relationships all my life. If I'm really creating my reality why would I put myself through such hardship? It would be so much easier to have a nice, relaxed life with lots of money in the bank and a stable, loving family.*

A: You would think so, wouldn't you? As a 3D human you might enjoy a quiet, simple life with all fun and no pain, but a higher vibrational light being who is born into this difficult dimension is looking for experiences, lessons to learn and challenges to overcome. Most of us don't come into a third dimensional physical reality for vacation, rather to go through a wide range of emotions and events. Throughout our many incarnations we gain knowledge and experience, accumulate what we call karma, and spend our lifetimes working through it.

Many people on Earth live difficult lives, but just because they are born into or find themselves in hardship it doesn't mean that they are destined to spend their entire life struggling. Once they start awakening and become conscious they can find all the information and the many tools that will help them raise their vibration. They can drop their karma and all the emotional baggage they've been carrying, not to mention all the things that no longer serve them, thus raising themselves out of their difficult circumstances. You too have the opportunity to learn how to raise and maintain your vibration, and that will greatly improve your life and circumstances.

When you find yourself wondering why so many people come in for such hard lives think about interviews you have seen with actors, many of whom talk about preferring challenging roles to simple, straightforward ones. Easy roles are boring, they tend to say, and they find the tough ones much more enjoyable, for those test one's acting abilities, talent and knowledge.

If you are dealing with a lot of issues in your life, may I suggest that you start working on your vibration and learn how to create your reality consciously instead of running on autopilot. If you put in the time and effort required and diligently apply what you've learned, you can turn your life around. You might not be able to solve all your issues, for you may have been born with certain parameters you cannot change (wheelchair bound, blind, caring for disabled relatives, etc). However, once you learn about our origin and understand the nature of reality, the dynamics of consciousness and energy and the roles of vibration and frequency, it will change your worldview and your attitude. You will be creating your reality fully conscious and aware, and that will make ALL the difference.

Q: *How do I know that I'm vibrating on a higher frequency?*

A: You notice that your life is beginning to quiet down. Instead of the usual ups and downs you begin to experience a relatively continuous evenness in your day to day existence. Your emotions quiet down as well and you no longer feel a slave to them. You get emotionally and in many other ways on an even keel. You find yourself drawn towards information that will instruct you how to keep raising your vibration and how to become conscious in your reality. You lose interest in ego based activities, comparisons, arguments, conflicts of any kinds and develop a desire to be of service to others, to humanity and to your planet. You become conscious of how your words and actions affect your environment. You notice that "problematic" people around you either quiet down or disappear from your life and you start gravitating towards people of higher vibration. You begin to feel an inner peace that wasn't there before, and as your thoughts quiet down life becomes calmer. You start listening to yourself more than to others, because you are beginning to trust your inner voice. You become conscious of synchronicities occurring in your life that are helping you find solutions to issues you are dealing with and placing you in places and situations that bring you what you asked for.

Believe me, you will know. Once I started to consciously and actively work on raising my vibration, the quality of my life changed considerably. Seeing people around me change with me was a much appreciated bonus because I didn't want to lose anybody. So get going and keep at it! It takes effort and a lot of work, but it will be all worth it.

Q: *What is the endgame here? What happens after we reach a certain frequency?*

A: What I understand based on my many years of research, study and personal experience is that as we are continuously raising our frequency we are slowly melding with - or embodying - our Higher Self, which is a multi-dimensional part of us in the higher dimensions. And as we are doing it en masse, humanity will ascend to the higher realms.

As others before me have described it, our multi-dimensional being is like one of those Russian doll-in-a-dolls called Matryoshka. Imagine that every doll in the stack is you in a different dimension. The outer one is the 3D you, that is the only one that is visible. The rest of them are all hidden from you because they are non-physical, but they are also you. As you are raising your vibration you get into higher frequencies, and at one point you reach the frequency of the next doll in the stack which is your Higher Self, and you meld into one. To be more precise, the veil between the two will disappear and you will be able to finally recognize the part of you that was always there, connected to you but out of sight. That's why you have always felt separate from it. You will embody your Higher Self and therefore you will become more of you. So basically I expect that by reaching a high enough frequency we will be reunited with our Higher Selves and continue creating our reality together, until the rest of humanity catches up and we all graduate to 5D, the point we originally started our Earth experiment from eons ago.

I know that this is a pretty simplistic way to describe it, but I find that this explanation of something so complex that we don't have a proper concept of it is fairly easy to imagine, so we can try to understand it.

If we are talking about Matryoshka and multidimensionality, I'm going to go out on a limb here and say that every time I think about Hindu goddesses with their multiple arms, I am reminded of our multidimensional nature in the multiverse and the many selves of us that exist in an infinite number of frequencies and realities. I imagine that I am the Goddess, and every set of arms of mine represents different lives I'm living in both physical and non-physical realities. They are all "separate" lives, but all of them stem from the one entity that is *Me*.

As for 5D, I have not just heard from people who experienced it, I also found myself shifting into it for a short time several times. I was in my backyard one day on the deck, taking clothes off my portable clothes dryer and folding them, when I noticed that something changed around me. I looked up and saw that the colours were different everywhere. The grass was super green, the sky was intensely blue and my entire garden gleamed with strong, vibrant colours. At first I didn't know what I was seeing, but soon it dawned on me that I was possibly looking at the hues of the 5D world.

The next time this happened I was out for a walk in a nearby park, feeling the natural high of being in nature, when once again I found myself in a souped up version of my reality with its incredibly lively and sparkling colours. Just like the first time the whole experience lasted a mere 20-30 seconds, and then I was once again back in my usual environment.

Q: *If you know so much about how to keep your vibration high and create your reality consciously, how come you are not a millionaire living in a mansion on a tropical island?*

A: Reading this book you might think that I have it all figured out and my life is perfect, but that's not exactly the case. I am still learning because there is always more to know and am still making "mistakes" as I go about my life. Sometimes I fall back into old habits, ignore the nagging feeling that is trying to warn me of something, and I don't always recognize an opportunity when it presents itself. However, at one point I always wake up, shake my head at my silliness and go forward with my eyes open. Sometimes

I still find myself stumped at some of my less desirable creations and work on finding the reason for them in my own belief system or attitude. Thankfully those are few and far between these days. The unpredictability of the past is gone, the surprises are few. Nevertheless, I am still a student as well as a teacher because the learning is never over. There were times in my life when I thought I finally had a good grasp on what life is all about and our roles in it. Then I learned new things and understood concepts and ideas that I didn't "get" before. So no matter how knowledgeable I may believe myself to be, there are always higher levels in front of me. Therefore I remain a student of life and a teacher of knowledge I've already acquired.

As for being rich, believe it or not, I have never dreamed of becoming a millionaire or living in a mansion. Not even a castle and I like those because I still love fairy tales. I very much enjoy the tropics though so trips to nice, warm places with ancient ruins are still in my future plans. Seriously though, it is interesting that so many people still believe that everyone wants to be rich, live in big houses, drive fancy cars and live a life of luxury. When we are young many of us do dream about it, but my experience is that as I got further on my spiritual path into the higher vibrations and left the mindset of 3D behind, my desires turned more towards service and gratitude. I found myself happy with my family and my lot in life, and my goal became wanting to help others enjoy what I have. And that is not millions of dollars in the bank, prestige, power or luxury. It's just a life of peace, creating and enjoying what I envision for my future, enough money to live a fulfilling life on, and participating in the greatest shift of our times, the ascension of humanity into the higher realms.

*Chapter 14*

**FINAL WORDS**

Dear Reader, I hope you have enjoyed this book with the examples I have taken from my own life and my personal experiences. I have to admit that although after all of these decades of learning, experimenting, practising, and having the confidence to say that I am skilled at conscious reality creation, I still feel amazed every time I bring a new dream into reality. Once you learn how to raise and maintain your vibration so you offer high frequency thoughts, actions and attitudes to the Universe to match, and use the tools and methods of creating your reality consciously, it feels rather like the secrets of successful living had been handed to you on a silver platter. As you keep learning, practising and getting excellent results you will get more and more confident with your skill, and will have no reason whatsoever to doubt your abilities and the outcomes of your efforts.

I have spent over two decades studying the nature of reality and the many different tools and methods that are used to successfully create and navigate one's personal world. I trust that my knowledge and experience I filled this book with will be of assistance to those who are on their journey of awakening. If you feel that this is your path and you are ready to awaken I suggest that you set the intention to do so. If you are reading this book though I think you already have. I wish you success, love and peace on your journey.

Ildiko Olah

# ABOUT THE AUTHOR

Ildiko Olah has spent the last twenty years walking the path of awakening: the exploration of her own Self and origin, her role in the creation of her life and the discovery of her life purpose.

Ildiko has been passionately science minded in her youth and was therefore closed to spiritual and paranormal ideas, until a mystical experience during a road trip in Arizona triggered her interest in reincarnation and other metaphysical concepts. During her journey of awakening she studied and experimented with projections of consciousness and different methods of conscious reality creation. As she learned more and more about herself and how she fit into the fabric of creation, she found her purpose. She knew that she was a teacher but had no idea what she was supposed to teach. It wasn't until one day in January 2023 that she experienced a moment of illumination when she realized the amount of spiritual knowledge, wisdom and experience she has amassed over her two decade long journey, and how she could share it all with those who are going through their own awakening.

*The Power of the Awakened Human* is Ildiko's first book. She wrote it in the hope that it would provide guidance for others on their own journey of self discovery and spiritual awakening.

Ildiko is still a student as well as a teacher, for learning and self discovery are never over. She is a lover of books, music, peace, long walks and hiking in nature. Where ever there is a patch of green or where water flows, she goes. She is an immigrant from Hungary, has two grown sons, and now lives in beautiful Northern Ontario, Canada with her husband of 37 years.

Please visit the Author's website at www.ildikoolah.com.

www.ingramcontent.com/pod-product-compliance
Lightning Source LLC
LaVergne TN
LVHW021708060526
838200LV00050B/2561